David Bland was born in Hartlepool, Cleveland in 1945. After leaving school in 1963, he worked in the Civil Service and in the SPCK Bookshop in Durham until 1967, and then trained as a teacher. In 1972, he took a post teaching Religious Education at the John Ferneley High School, Melton Mowbray, and later became a member of the Humanities Department.

He enjoys a variety of hobbies, including singing, and listening to all types of music. He is an avid reader and collector of books and also enjoys travelling, visiting Wales and Guernsey at every possible opportunity.

ALED JONES

WALKING ON AIR

Aled's own story as told to
David Bland
with a Foreword by
Stuart Burrows

Fontana/Collins

First published in 1986 by Fontana Paperbacks
8 Grafton Street, London W1X 3LA

Photoset by Rowland Phototypesetting Ltd
Bury St Edmunds Suffolk
Made and printed in Great Britain by
William Collins Sons & Co. Ltd, Glasgow

Contents

For Aled – whose voice 'reaches to the heart'.

Foreword

When he first appeared as one of my guests at St David's Hall, Cardiff, in January 1985 it was apparent that, even for one so young, Aled Jones had all the qualities which breed success. His confidence, natural ability, enthusiasm and musicianship, allied to his glorious voice, have thrilled and endeared him to millions of people. He is blessed with a natural charm and has confidently taken his enormous success with admirable modesty. Artistic integrity is at least as meaningful to this young man as gathering public acclaim. I am sure we all wish his future career in music to be as happy and successful as it has been to date.

STUART BURROWS

Preface

In May 1983, a lady member of the congregation of Bangor Cathedral wrote to the Sain Recording Company of Llandwrog, near Caernarfon: 'There is a boy in the Choir at Bangor Cathedral who has a truly remarkable voice.'

Nobody could have foretold what the consequences of that letter would be. Aled Jones is now an international celebrity. His records have sold in hundreds of thousands. He has received three Gold Discs and had a recent Top Twenty hit with the single 'Walking in the Air', from which the title of this book is derived. He has been seen on television all over the world and has sung on radio and given many interviews. What an amazing achievement for a fifteen-year-old boy from Anglesey.

Many people, famous and not so famous, in fact people from all walks of life have found themselves enriched, their spirits uplifted, and have even been moved to tears by the unique and wonderful sound of Aled's voice.

Aled and his parents, Sain Recordings and the BBC have received thousands of letters from people all over the world. Some of these are included in this book. Other tributes have come from the well-known people who have worked with Aled, whether on TV or radio, in the recording studio, or on the concert platform. They testify to the high place Aled holds in their affection by their willingness to contribute to this book.

It has been a great privilege for me to be able to honour Aled's success in this way and I offer this appreciation in words and pictures to his many admirers the world over.

David Bland,
February 1986

CHAPTER ONE

Early days

'Build me a son whose heart will be clear, whose goal will be high: a son who will master himself before he seeks to master other men; one who will learn to laugh, yet never forget how to weep; one who will reach into the future, yet never forget the past.

'And after all these things are his, add, I pray, enough of a sense of humour so that he may always be serious, yet never take himself too seriously. Give him humility, so that he may always remember the simplicity of true greatness, the open mind of true wisdom, the meekness of true strength.

'Then I, his father, will dare to whisper, "I have not lived in vain."'

General Douglas MacArthur (1880–1964)

Aled Jones was born in St David's Hospital, Bangor on 29 December 1970. His mother, Nest, was an infant-school teacher; she took leave of absence when Aled was born, returning to school seven weeks later. During schooltime, the baby Aled was looked after by his grandparents. Both sets of grandparents were musical and Aled heard a lot of singing at home. From a very early age Aled showed an interest in music and loved a family sing-song, when Nest's mother would play the piano.

When asked where Aled got his voice from, his father, Derek, says, 'He doesn't get it from me, I assure you. I'm absolutely tone deaf–I don't play any instruments and I can't sing.' Derek agrees, however that Nest can play the piano and sing a bit, although he doesn't think she is very musical. Nest's family come from Caernarfon and Anglesey and have always been musical, and Derek's family are quite prominent in the local 'musical world'.

By the time Aled was two years old, he had developed an ability to reproduce accurately a variety of the sounds he had heard, whether it was someone singing, noises in the kitchen or the growl of a car.

Aled started school in the infant section of Llandegfan Primary School in September 1975. Usually, there are tearful farewells from both child and mother on the first day at school, but not so in Aled's case. As well as being 'Mam' in the home, Nest also taught Aled during his early years at primary school and the headteacher at the school, Edward Morris Jones, refers to Nest as 'a most imaginative and caring class teacher'.

By the summer of 1978, Aled's mother could be forgiven for giving a little sigh of relief! She had enjoyed every minute of her three years with Aled and his little friends, but from now on someone else would be taking over, in school at least. Edward Morris Jones takes up the story: 'My own daughter, Awen, joined the class in the summer of 1978, so from then on I had an increasingly personal interest in the group taught by our friend and deputy, Glynne Williams. The medium of instruction for the children in the group was Welsh, but living in an area such as ours in the 1980s, these children had no difficulty with their second language, English. It was a good group of children with many varied interests between them. There was, however, one main common factor between them all–they could and did sing well!'

At the age of six, Aled sang in his first public concert at Llandegfan Parish Hall. He remembers the occasion well: 'I used to hate singing before that and I just went, sang, and the applause was great. After that, I just loved singing.'

From then on, in the daily services at Llandegfan Primary School, you could not help noticing one group of six-year-old children. They really enjoyed their singing, led by an energetic, fair-haired little lad– Aled, whose crystal-clear voice was noticed, not only by teachers and friends, but by his peers as well. He was thrilled to bits when it came to his turn to sing a verse on his own before everyone joined in the chorus. Edward Morris Jones remembers, 'Children are good at recognizing that there is something special about a performance: the clear voice of a small boy. The soloist Aled was beginning to make his appearance.' Aled was an obvious candidate to be encouraged to take part in solo competitions. The teacher responsible for music development at the school, Miss Elsie Francis, felt that he was one to watch and foster carefully. As it turned out, her judgement was proved so right.

From the age of six, Aled went to St Tegfan's Sunday School in Llandegfan every week. Canon Meurig Foulkes, Rector of the parish, remembers him well: 'On occasions such as the Parish Communion and in nativity plays, Aled could be relied upon to take an active and intelligent part. He possessed then a good speaking and singing voice, which, as a future member of the Cathedral Choir in Bangor, he was able to develop and exercise to the full.'

One of the Sunday School teachers, Mrs Betty Evans, recommended that his parents send Aled to the Bangor Cathedral Choir, but they did not follow up her recommendation as they felt Aled was too young and the Choir would be too demanding.

Aled's talents were developing in a variety of ways. He took part in various sports–cycling, swimming, sailing and football–and from 1977 to 1980 he was a member of the 1st Llandegfan Cub Scout Group, obtaining a number of proficiency badges as well as singing and taking part in all their shows. In December 1980, Aled sang a lullaby carol under the Christmas tree at school, recorded by BBC Wales. Christmas

Left: Llandegfan Primary School football team.

Below: at the helm of his father's boat

Below right: catching whitebait on the Lleyn Peninsular

Right: the big catch

1981 saw Aled taking the leading role in the Andrew Lloyd Webber/ Tim Rice hit musical *Joseph and the Amazing Technicolour Dreamcoat*—a memorable occasion during his final year at primary school. In 1982, during his last year at primary school, he also took part in a local Music Festival production, *Huw Cymunod*, which was a light opera about a strong man from Anglesey.

Left: the cast of *Huw Cymunod*

At the age of seven, Aled entered the Urdd (Youth) National Eisteddfod in the area preliminary round, but failed to be staged. Many Eisteddfodau followed, with mixed success, but in 1979 Aled won first prize at the Village Eisteddfod at Bontnewydd near Caernarfon (his father's home village).

In 1981, Aled's parents felt that he needed specialist training for Eisteddfodau. He started being trained by Mrs Nia Wyn Jones, a contralto who was herself a winner of numerous National Eisteddfodau, including the coveted Blue Riband Award. As a result of this training, Aled had a double success in 1982 in the Anglesey Area Urdd Eisteddfod at Amlwch, winning the Solo and Cerdd Dant (accompanied by harp) events at 'under 12'. He went on to win both classes in the Urdd National Eisteddfod finals at Pwllheli the same year.

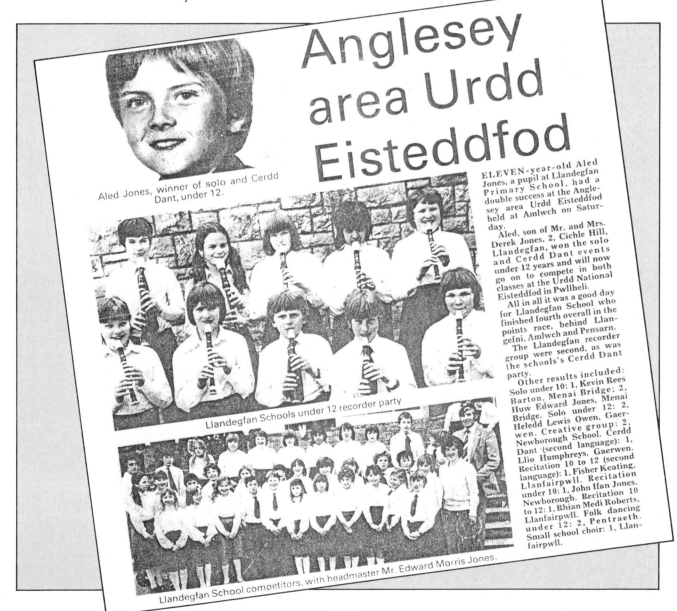

Anglesey area Urdd Eisteddfod

Aled Jones, winner of solo and Cerdd Dant, under 12.

ELEVEN-year-old Aled Jones, a pupil at Llandegfan Primary School, had a double success at the Anglesey area Urdd Eisteddfod held at Amlwch on Saturday.

Aled, son of Mr. and Mrs. Derek Jones, 2, Cichle Hill, Llandegfan, won the solo and Cerdd Dant events under 12 years and will now go on to compete in both classes at the Urdd National Eisteddfod in Pwllheli.

All in all it was a good day for Llandegfan School who finished fourth overall in the points race, behind Llangefni, Amlwch and Pensarn.

The Llandegfan recorder group were second, as was the schools's Cerdd Dant party.

Other results included:
Solo under 10: 1, Kevin Rees Barton, Menai Bridge; 2, Huw Edward Jones, Menai Bridge. Solo under 12: 2, Heledd Lewis Owen, Gaerwen. Creative group: 2, Newborough School. Cerdd Dant (second language): 1, Llio Humphreys, Gaerwen. Recitation 10 to 12 (second language): 1, Fisher Keating, Llanfairpwll. Recitation under 10: 1, John Ifan Jones, Newborough. Recitation 10 to 12: 1, Rhian Medi Roberts, Llanfairpwll. Folk dancing under 12: 2, Pentraeth. Small school choir: 1, Llanfairpwll.

Llandegfan Schools under 12 recorder party

Llandegfan School competitors, with headmaster Mr. Edward Morris Jones.

Left: Aled wears his Eisteddfod prize ribbon

Right: Aled and a fellow prize-winner at the 1982 Eisteddfod

After this, Aled no longer competed at Eisteddfodau, because his parents felt that now that he was beginning to make a name for himself as a concert singer, as well as on records and television, other competitors might well feel at a disadvantage with someone whose name was so well known among the adjudicators.

In December 1982, Aled gained success in other directions by passing Grade 3 Piano with a Distinction, obtaining 136 marks out of 150, under the tuition of Andrew Goodwin. Aled's piano teacher is now Annette Bryn Parri, who has also been his accompanist for the last two years (1984–5). But she has recently found that Aled has become so busy with other commitments that, 'I suppose he's had *three* piano lessons during the past year [1985]. Even when he is piano playing his musicality is apparent–for example, his feel for musical phrases is something that comes quite naturally.' She goes on, 'In rehearsal, Aled and I do not have a teacher-pupil relationship: it tends to be 'teamwork', and that teamwork enables him to appear on the stage with confidence–not having to worry about what the accompanist is going to do next!'

CHAPTER TWO

Cathedral chorister

'. . . once you've joined the Cathedral Choir, you belong to it . . . I was doing a lot of work for the BBC and so on at the time, and so I eventually had to leave. I minded it a lot . . .'
(Aled – 'The Treble', *Omnibus*)

John Hugh Thomas, Conductor of the BBC Welsh Chorus, explains the opportunities available for boy singers in Wales: 'In Wales, boy sopranos – or trebles – can generally be divided into two distinct categories. There are those who are trained in a good church or cathedral choir, where their general musicianship may be brought to a very high level, and there are those whose musical experience and awareness is developed largely through public appearances as soloists or competitors in music festivals.

'Regular singing in a good church choir tends to develop a very different kind of singer from the one whose gifts are sharpened by performing as a soloist or by competing on the Eisteddfod platform. The former, if he has the ability to absorb and respond to the training, may develop considerable musical skills: a good ear, a keen sense of pitch, a knowledge of musical styles and the ability to read music accurately and fluently. The second type, if he is blessed with a strong voice and a good temperament, may develop a distinctive musical personality, but lack some of those skills acquired by the church chorister.

'Very few boys seem to have succeeded in combining both worlds successfully. Aled Jones is one who has succeeded, and has done so spectacularly.'

The choirboys in Bangor Cathedral are recruited from the primary schools of the area and the cathedral clergy are greatly indebted to headteachers and staff for their assistance. Some years ago, Miss Elsie Francis, a worshipper at the Cathedral, persuaded one of her pupils to apply for an audition. Initially, Aled's parents approached Andrew Goodwin (Organist and Master of the Choristers at Bangor Cathedral) with a view to Aled receiving piano tuition. When Aled came to audition for piano lessons, Andrew Goodwin asked him to sing and realized that he had a very promising voice. (He had previously been told by one of Aled's schoolteachers that he showed evidence of vocal ability.)

In the spring of 1980, when he was nine, Aled became a probationer in the Cathedral Choir. Bright-faced and fair-haired, he was an

Practising Stainer's
Crucifixion

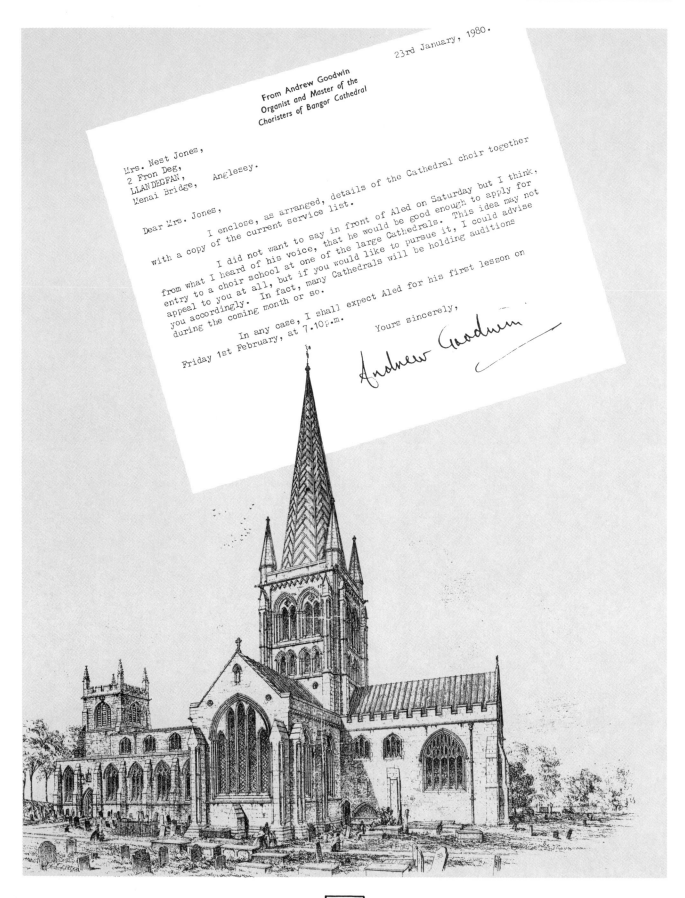

23rd January, 1980.

From Andrew Goodwin
Organist and Master of the
Choristers of Bangor Cathedral

Mrs. Nest Jones,
2 Fron Deg,
LLANDEGFAN,
Menai Bridge, Anglesey.

Dear Mrs. Jones,

I enclose, as arranged, details of the Cathedral choir together with a copy of the current service list.

I did not want to say in front of Aled on Saturday but I think, from what I heard of his voice, that he would be good enough to apply for entry to a choir school at one of the large Cathedrals. This idea may not appeal to you at all, but if you would like to pursue it, I could advise you accordingly. In fact, many Cathedrals will be holding auditions during the coming month or so.

In any case, I shall expect Aled for his first lesson on Friday 1st February, at 7.10p.m.

Yours sincerely,

Andrew Goodwin

ordinary boy, as mischievous as the next and full of life and energy. It was soon obvious that Aled had an exceptionally good voice, and in due course he took his full place in the Choir. He made good progress and in a comparatively short time became a soloist. Andrew Goodwin remembers this well: 'He was an exceedingly nervous chorister, but was given a great deal of encouragement and assistance by his fellow choristers and the organ scholars. As he gained experience, his assurance of musical style became very obvious; not only was there a fine voice in evidence, but also a real sense of musical purpose and style in all his singing.'

The Dean of Bangor speaks highly of the training that choristers receive from Andrew Goodwin: 'Mr Goodwin devotes a great deal of time and talent to the boys, training them with discipline and patience.

Below: rehearsal with Andrew Goodwin

He does not have favourites and Aled was treated no differently from the other boys. However, it became increasingly obvious that Aled's voice was improving beyond recognition through the training he was receiving, and it was good to hear Aled pay tribute to the grounding he received in the Cathedral Choir [on *Omnibus*].' Aled confirms the very high standards expected from the choristers: 'Mr Goodwin was really, really strict. If we messed around, there'd be trouble. We were there to work, we just couldn't make mistakes—everything had to be perfect.'

Many pictures appeared, showing Aled in his chorister's robes with an angelic look on his face. However, James Griffiths, the Honorary Assistant Organist at Bangor Cathedral, was not taken in by Aled's innocent appearance: 'Let not his angelic visage lead anyone to think that he is so! I have had to tell him off quite a number of times for slight acts of misbehaviour in the Choir room. When all the boys were standing round the grand piano, rehearsing a service or anthem, little acts of foot-stamping or pushing, again with that angelic look!'

In an interview in *Woman's Own*, 25 August 1985, Aled makes his own confession: 'We used to throw books at each other under the piano to try and make each other laugh. Once, some people put sticky stuff under the notes of the piano so that when the Choirmaster tried to play, they wouldn't work.' (Possibly this was one way to practise singing 'unaccompanied'!)

Despite the usual choirboy misdemeanours, James Griffiths was much impressed by Aled's voice, musicianship and qualities of leadership: 'I was a conductor of the Choir on many occasions. Aled could be relied on absolutely to "come in" and to lead the others in some difficult passage and this was a great comfort to me as conductor.'

Mrs Hefina Orwig Evans (who later wrote to Sain Recordings) has many memories of Aled's days in the Choir: 'At the Choral Eucharist in Bangor Cathedral, when Aled used to take the solo part in the "Sanctus" it was something unforgettable—I don't think he has ever sung better than he sang then. And there was a memorable carol service in the Cathedral when Aled sang the first verse of "Once In Royal David's City" at the back of the Cathedral.' When asked whether there was anything particularly 'different' about Aled, Mrs Orwig Evans said there wasn't: 'There was nothing except that he looked so sweet with his blond hair. He was a very ordinary boy—very, very mischievous—always knocking conkers down after the service, and things like that.'

Dr George Guest, Organist and Master of the Choristers at St John's College, Cambridge, and a native of Bangor himself, describes Aled's unique gifts: 'Of course, he's one of the best trebles that I've ever heard. I think the thing about treble singing is this: you have to have three attributes. You have to have a very good voice—of course, many boys have got good voices; you have to have also an innate kind of musicianship; and then the third attribute is being virtually nerveless,

without nerves, when performing in public. Now, many boys have one or two of these characteristics. Aled has all three, and that is really the reason why he is such an outstanding treble.'

In the summer of 1983, the Cathedral Choir were to embark on a short tour of West Germany to sing in various churches as part of the commemoration of Martin Luther. This entailed raising funds and arranging preliminary concerts, one of which was a Singing Festival in the Cathedral in which one of Wales' leading choirs, the Penrhyn Male Voice Choir, took part. James Griffiths remembers the occasion: 'I well remember the reaction of the Male Choir and the large congregation when they heard Aled and the Cathedral Choir singing Mendelssohn's "Hear My Prayer". Many in that congregation had never heard Aled before but they were all amazed at the quality of his voice and the professionalism of his performance.' Aled was a soloist for the Choir's recitals during their tour of Germany; he held the official position of third chorister. They set out on their nine-day tour on 13 July, and sang in Soest, Mannheim, Speyer and Worms. The tour was a great success.

At this time, Andrew Goodwin was fortunate to have the assistance of Elizabeth Le Grove as an Organ Scholar. She was able to give Aled a great deal of help, especially during the years 1982 and 1983. She was able to build up his confidence and made a valuable contribution in teaching him 'Hear My Prayer' and *Elijah*, both by Mendelssohn. Elizabeth played the organ on the German tour and conducted the Choir at the Christmas Concert in Penrhyn Castle.

The Dean of Bangor reflects on Aled's development as a chorister at this time: 'It was during this period and on the German tour that Aled's voice matured and the benefits of good training bore fruit. His singing and obvious enjoyment of his art captured audiences wherever the Choir sang, and concerts held later that year and at Christmas proved unforgettable experiences.'

During 1984 the media discovered Aled, and calls on his time made it increasingly difficult for him to fulfil his obligations to both Choir and Cathedral. Aled himself explains the problem: 'At the Cathedral, practices were happening for services, four or five times a week, and I had to miss them. When I started missing choir practices every week, really, I sensed that something was going to happen, because once you've joined the Cathedral Choir, you belong to it; you're not allowed to do anything else. I was doing a lot of work for the BBC and so on at that time and so I eventually had to leave. I minded it a lot because I was missing all my friends there. I'd made really good friends and I'd been there four and a half years and it just had to finish so suddenly. It was a choice really, I had to give up something—leaving the Choir was the cost of being the soloist.'

The Dean of Bangor, speaking for everyone at the Cathedral, felt that Aled's departure from the Choir was a great loss, but inevitable

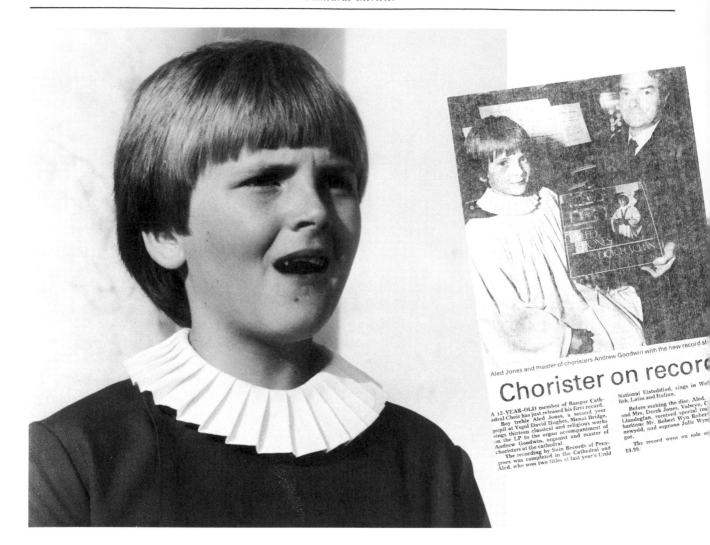

Aled Jones and master of choristers Andrew Goodwin with the new record sl

Chorister on record

A 12-YEAR-OLD member of Bangor Cathedral Choir has just released his first record.
Boy treble Aled Jones, a second year pupil at Ysgol David Hughes, Menai Bridge, sings thirteen classical and religious works on the LP to the organ accompaniment of Andrew Goodwin, organist and master of choristers at the cathedral.
The recording by Sain Records of Penygroes was completed in the Cathedral and Aled, who won two titles at last year's Urdd

National Eisteddfod, sings in Welsh, Latin and Italian.
Before making the disc, Aled, and Mrs. Derek Jones, Valwyn, C Llandegfan, received special tra baritone Mr. Robert Wyn Rober newydd, and soprano Julie Wyn gor.
The record went on sale o £4.99.

under the circumstances: 'The parting of the ways was a sad occasion for us at the Cathedral and for Aled and his family. We are glad that we had his talent to help our Cathedral carry on its ancient tradition of praise and prayer; glad too that so many millions have since been thrilled by so marvellous a voice.

'When his busy schedule allows, Aled still worships in the Cathedral and it is good to see that fame and success have not spoiled him, and that he remains (although older) still the same fresh-faced and fair-haired youngster we first knew.'

It is fitting that a final tribute to Aled's time in the Cathedral Choir should come from his own Bishop, the Bishop of Bangor: 'When I became Bishop of Bangor at the beginning of 1982, Aled Jones was already a well-established member of the Choir of Bangor Cathedral, and it was always a delight and inspiration to listen to the cadences of his rich voice ascending to the heights. Since then, Aled has become world famous, has achieved fame through the media of radio, television and records. Others more competent than myself will be able to pay tribute to the musical qualities of his voice.

VIRGIN RECORDS

'There are many who have been captivated by the natural, unaffected and self-effacing presentation of his character in interviews and appearances before vast audiences. I would want to pay tribute to Aled, not as a soloist, for his beautiful boy-soprano voice is by nature only a temporary phenomenon, but as a moral example we would all do well to emulate. The demands made on Aled from a multiplicity of outside sources meant that he had to be excluded from the Choir he loved so dearly. If he were unable to attend practices, this would not be fair to his fellow choristers. Aled realized that, and bore no resentment. The world-acclaimed soloist was not expecting preferential treatment.

'To me this is a moral jewel to be treasured above anything else in such an age as this, and for this reason alone I am more than pleased to be granted the privilege of adding these comments to this appreciation of Aled Jones.'

In 1983, Aled's professional engagements began to increase and his voice began to be heard more on the concert platform. One of the most significant performances took place on 17 March in the Prichard-Jones

Hall of the University College of North Wales, Bangor. Together with the choir, singers and orchestra of University College, Aled took his place in the company of such well-known soloists as Janet Price, Margaret Cable, Neil Jenkins and Ian Caddy, and played a significant part in a fine performance of Mendelssohn's oratorio *Elijah*. Aled had been recommended for the solo treble part by Pam Wilkinson, and was asked to audition for the part before Wyn Thomas, the Conductor and Musical Director. Elizabeth Le Grove had played the piano for his audition.

In October 1983, Robert Wyn Roberts, a graduate of the Royal Northern College of Music in Manchester, was asked by a friend and fellow graduate of the same college, Julie Wynne, to listen to a twelve-year-old boy treble named Aled Jones. Julie had been asked by Andrew Goodwin if she would be prepared to take him on as a singing pupil. He was still relatively unknown; apart from a few concert performances, his experience had been largely confined to the Bangor Cathedral Choir and competitive Eisteddfodau. Robert Wyn Roberts remembers how Aled first impressed him: 'I well remember the basic shyness that veiled the personality within. Although his vocal range was limited, certain attributes of his uneven, inexperienced singing did impress me, particularly the ringing quality of his glowing upper high register. The first step was to discourage all bluster and concentrate on even singing within a phrase and to make the voice sound natural.'

Although Aled had been taught with great discipline and dedication by Andrew Goodwin while he was in the Cathedral Choir, and his subsequent success owes a lot to the grounding he received from him, now that he was beginning to make his mark outside the Choir, it was felt that his singing technique could be improved further. Robert and Julie agreed to take on Aled as a pupil and were immediately plunged into the world of the media, for Aled was shortly to appear on his first television programme (for the Welsh Channel, S4C). This was to be recorded on 17 October in the Parish Church of St Mary and St Nicholas, Beaumaris, for the Welsh hymn programme, *Dechreu Canu, Dechreu Canmol*.

Canon Meurig Foulkes, Rector of Beaumaris and Llandegfan, explains how Aled came to be chosen: 'The producer of the programme was anxious that I should recommend a soloist with local connections. Having heard Aled sing in the Cathedral on several occasions, I had no hesitation in suggesting that he be approached.'

It was very appropriate therefore that Aled's first television appearance should be in his home parish. Aled sang two songs, César Franck's 'Panis Angelicus' and the lovely 'Pie Jesu' from Fauré's *Requiem* (sung in Welsh). Despite the strangeness of it all, Aled coped very well. He also had to put up with the attentions of a gang of schoolboys outside, who had unfortunately caught a glimpse of Aled in his 'dress', as they called his cassock and surplice.

DOUGLAS GOWAN

CHAPTER THREE

On record

'Not long after, they came to the Cathedral to record my voice. They came in a mobile recording studio – I was singing inside the Cathedral and they were recording in the van, and that's how the first record was produced.'

(Aled – 'The Treble', *Omnibus*)

When Aled was singing a solo in the Sunday services at the Cathedral, his mother used to bring a small tape-recorder with her and record whatever he sang, even if it was just a line or two. As Aled's voice developed, members of the Cathedral congregation began to take an interest and suggested to Aled's mother that she should have his voice recorded properly. Among them was Mrs Hefina Orwig Evans, the widow of a former Residentiary Canon of the Cathedral. Aled's mother hadn't done anything further about a proper recording and so Mrs Evans decided to take action herself. In May 1983, she wrote to Sain Recordings, a local company based at Llandwrog near Caernarfon who specialized in Welsh artists and Welsh language recordings. Her original letter is reproduced below, translated from the Welsh:

Dear Friends,

A twelve-year-old boy from Ysgol David Hughes, Menai Bridge, called Aled Jones, has a special voice. He won First Prize in the Urdd National Eisteddfod last year and First Prize for the Cerdd Dant solo.

He is the chief soloist with Bangor Cathedral Choir and the Choir will be singing on the 500th Anniversary of Martin Luther's birth in Worms in July, with Aled as soloist.

On Sunday night, there was a 'Festival of Song' in the Cathedral and Aled, with the Choir, sang 'Hear My Prayer' quite outstandingly. I thought that night what a tragedy it would be for his voice to break and there be no record of him. Before he went to Ysgol David Hughes, Aled was a pupil at Llandegfan, where Edward Morris Jones is headmaster, and he could confirm he has a special voice.

I wonder if you are interested? I am not a relative of his and there is no connection other than that I have this great desire to have a record of his voice.

Yours truly,
Hefina Orwig Evans (Mrs)

On a later occasion, Mrs Evans was asked to re-write the letter to Sain for the purposes of filming the *Omnibus* programme, 'The Treble'. On this occasion she wrote: 'There is a boy who sings in the Bangor Cathedral Choir who has a truly remarkable voice that *reaches to the heart*' – a phrase which so beautifully conveys the wonderful feeling in Aled's voice and how it can affect people.

Mrs Evans and now the Sain Recording Company were to play a fundamental part in Aled's success. Very soon after receiving Mrs Evans' letter, a representative of Sain visited Aled and his parents. At that time, Sain had no boy soprano on their books, and they were looking for one to fill the gap in their catalogue. They planned to issue a long-playing record with Aled singing on one side and another treble

With his singing teachers, Julie Wynne and Robert Wyn Roberts

on the other side. For various reasons, it was not possible to do this, so they decided to 'risk' the whole record on Aled. For a small company, it was quite a large 'risk', but arrangements went ahead. The LP was recorded in Bangor Cathedral on two evenings in November 1983, in unusual conditions. To get the best results, it was necessary for Aled to sing from the pulpit into the main body of the Cathedral. This meant that he was unable to see Andrew Goodwin on the Cathedral organ, and created problems of synchronization between voice and organ. The problem was solved in an interesting way: Aled sang from the pulpit facing Robert, and Julie relayed the beat to Robert from the organist.

Despite the recording difficulties, Sain, on hearing the master tapes, had no hesitation in going ahead and releasing the record. The LP 'Diolch â Chân' (Thanks in Song) first appeared in the shops shortly before Christmas 1983. It included well-known items from the treble repertoire and Aled sang in Welsh, English, Latin and Italian. Much credit must go to Aled's singing teachers, who prepared him very thoroughly for this and subsequent records and taught him to sing in a variety of languages.

Robert Wynne Roberts comments on this first recording, '"Diolch â Chân" shows a voice that is fresh and natural. Aled's naïve approach also enhances the overall purity. The results that were achieved were quite remarkable, although several aspects of his singing had yet to mature. The end product is a treasure and is the epitome of poignancy.'

The record was given a pleasing review by Dr Gareth H. Lewis in the Journal of the Guild for the Promotion of Welsh Music:

> Since the days of the great Ernest Lough, there has been no shortage of recordings by boy sopranos. There were several distinguished Welsh boys who recorded in the 1930s (whatever became of Master John Gwilym Griffiths, the finest of all, I think?), but none, as far as I can recall, in recent years. Aled Jones, a Bangor Cathedral chorister with a number of competition successes behind him, more than adequately makes up for this deficiency.
>
> On his first record, he has chosen a formidably varied programme, taking in Handel, Schubert, Schumann, Mozart, Giordano's 'Caro Mio Ben', Franck's 'Panis Angelicus', the 'Pie Jesu' from Fauré's *Requiem*, two traditional songs and a hymn. He tackles them all with outstanding confidence. Unlike many boy trebles, Aled Jones almost invariably sings dead in tune, with generally commendable steadiness. His crisp attack, clear projection of the words and careful phrasing could serve as a model for some of the disappointingly slovenly adult singers I have heard in recent months . . . A delightful record which has given me a lot of pleasure.

At first, public reaction to the record was lukewarm, but quite soon, as articles and reviews began to appear, there was a gradual rise in sales. Shortly after the record was released, Dr George Guest described Aled's voice as 'one of the best examples of boy treble singing ever heard'. He later wrote to Aled, congratulating him on his album: 'There is nothing wrong with the record—solid intonation, sensitive and musical phrasing, and a voice that serves the music and the composer's wishes.' In playing the record to his own choir before practice sessions, Dr Guest described Aled's singing as 'an excellent example of singing at its best'.

For Aled, 1984 began significantly with a reference to him outside the borders of Wales. The *Church Times* of 13 January 1984 carried a picture of Aled, together with a short article explaining how a twelve-year-old choirboy from Anglesey had made his first record. This was virtually the first time that he had been mentioned nationally, and his fame was beginning to spread as Sain Recordings began to receive orders for his record from outside Wales.

In March, Derek and Nest, Aled's parents, were surprised to receive a telephone call from none other than BBC broadcaster, Richard Baker. He told Aled's parents that he would be playing Aled's record on 24 March on his radio programme, *Baker's Dozen*. 'As soon as I heard the record,' he recalls, 'I was convinced that here was a boy's voice of exceptional quality. It is rare for such a voice to be consistently good throughout its range, and comparisons with the legendary Ernest Lough quickly came to mind. I'd had a bit of a nudge towards playing the record in the shape of a letter from a neighbour of the Joneses and that was why I thought I'd ring them and tell them when I would include it. They were pleased, but I don't think unduly surprised, at my high opinion of Aled's voice! I have since rejoiced at his success and am delighted to hear that Aled remains unspoiled. Long may this be so.'

Aled remains unconvinced when comparisons are made between Ernest Lough and himself: 'Since this last year, everyone's been comparing me to Ernest Lough. I've listened to his record and he's really, really good, but I don't think that my voice is the same as his. Someone told me that he was still recording when he was sixteen years old.' (*Omnibus*)

Meanwhile, Aled continued his singing lessons with Robert and Julie and had a ready appetite and enthusiasm for new repertoire. In December 1983, shortly after 'Diolch â Chân' had appeared in the shops, Aled sang with Julie Wynne in the Choristers' Concert at the stately home of Penrhyn Castle, just outside Bangor. This gave him another chance to perform in front of an audience; the Great Hall at Penryhn was packed to bursting. His shyness was becoming a thing of

Aled with Robert

GERALLT LLEWELYN

the past and his two teachers had begun to test Aled's potential as an actor. His performance of Rossini's 'Cat Duet' with Julie was a resounding success, and he received his first standing ovation. Julie remembers it well: 'Performing with Aled was quite a task. He certainly made you work hard because, apart from his obviously beautiful voice, his angelic looks won over his audience even before he had opened his mouth.'

Aled with Hefin Elis at Sain

In January 1984, he willingly helped the cause of the ailing Bangor Pier by appearing in a Victorian Evening that had been organized to raise funds. As Julie recalls, 'We dressed Aled up and had a go at him with some stage make-up. The end result was something between Little Lord Fauntleroy and Richmal Crompton's William.'

Aled's first recording for Sain was such a success that during 1984, Sain finalized plans to make a second one. A selection of material was made, again in various languages, from the usual treble repertoire. The recording was made at the end of July, in two sessions. Like the first, it was made in Bangor Cathedral, but due to technical reasons it was not a success. Arrangements were then made to do the complete recording again, this time in Beaumaris Parish Church. This particular development was to show another aspect of Aled's character, namely, endurance! Despite plans to make the recording over a period of two days, it was completed in *one* session. Aled sang a total of fifteen songs – an amazing feat for one so young.

'Ave Maria' was released in November 1984 and soon became a popular choice for Christmas presents. Robert Wyn Roberts reflects on Aled's developing style: 'By the time of his second recording, a more experienced performer begins to emerge. The vocal range has stretched from the modest top A♭ of his first recording to the B above. He is now a master of phrasing and legato, dramatic yet sensitive, with an authority and confidence far beyond his years.'

After hearing 'Ave Maria', Dr George Guest from St John's College, Cambridge, wrote enthusiastically to Sain:

> Heartfelt thanks for sending Aled's second record to me. I enjoyed his first record, but I believe it is impossible to write about his new record without using words which imply a kind of perfection which is impossible in our imperfect world!
>
> Indeed, Aled's voice is something special and priceless, but he also brings something else to his performance, and that is his beautifully shaped and musical phrasing. Thus, he has the ability to communicate, through his interpretations, the essence of the song to his listeners in a very precise way. The new record deserves every success; it is excellent!

'Ave Maria', however, received a mixed reception; despite that, it has sold just as well as 'Diolch â Chân'. These two recordings from the small Welsh company based near Caernarfon are for many people the finest that Aled has made.

CHAPTER FOUR

Handel's *Jephtha*

'It was the first time that I'd sung with an orchestra. I was only supposed to sing a small part but Neville Marriner wanted me to sing both the recitative and the aria and so it was an extra bonus—quite large pieces, with an orchestra.'
(Aled—*John Dunn Show*, Radio 2, 19 July 1985)

After the success of Aled's first record, 'Diolch â Chân', the unexpected invitation to sing the part of the Angel in Handel's *Jephtha*, conducted by Neville Marriner, brought his talent to light on the professional stage. Hefin Owen, Music Producer at BBC Wales, had been let down by a boy treble two weeks before the proposed recording of *Jephtha* at St David's Hall in Cardiff on 28 April 1984. He happened to see Aled's record on sale at a Male Voice Choir Concert he went to. He bought the record and was obviously impressed: not long afterwards, Aled received a letter asking him to sing the part of the Angel. He was sent both the recitative and the aria to learn, but was told that he would only be asked to sing the recitative, as the aria would be too long. However, Aled's singing teachers, Robert Wyn Roberts and Julie Wynne, decided it would be in Aled's interests to learn both and he did so very successfully in the short space of time available for practice.

Julie takes up the story: 'I had arranged to meet Aled and his mother at St David's Hall on the day before the concert, for a listening with Neville Marriner. I had been staying with my friend Fiona, who is a music teacher in Bridgend but lives in Cardiff. She came with me to St David's Hall in case we had a chance to practise with a piano. We were lucky, and were shown into the Green Room where one was available. Fiona played through the pieces with Aled and we tightened up a few of the trills. Suddenly, Neville Marriner was brought in and introduced to us. Fiona's face was a picture of surprise. Her surprise was even greater when the conductor turned to her and said, "Shall we start the practice?" She had to play for Aled until the real accompanist turned up. She told me afterwards that she had been "scared to death". The rehearsal went so well and Aled so impressed Neville Marriner that he agreed to let Aled sing the aria as well as the recitative.'

Aled remembered the occasion for the *Omnibus* programme, 'The Treble': 'I wasn't really nervous when I confronted Mr Neville Marriner for the first time because I wasn't quite sure who he was. When Mr Marriner spoke to me the first time, he said "You'll be singing the recitative and there's no chance of you singing the aria,'' but he didn't stop me in between and I just asked the accompanist to carry on and I said I'd give it a go.'

After the practice was over, Neville Marriner gave his opinion of Aled's voice and suitability for the part of the Angel: 'Quite remarkable—I think one of the things that usually destroys your confidence in boys' voices is that they obviously lack experience. They usually sing immensely sharp and nothing comes out the same twice. This [Aled's voice] shows extraordinary experience—suddenly you have a mature personality behind a very secure voice and I think perhaps we could now try to capitalize on this and introduce him into the plot. Normally, you don't really want too much of the Angel here, but I think I'd like to try and keep him in.'

The next day was the day of the performance. Julie sat in the audience with Aled during the first part of *Jephtha*. He was very quiet and was obviously nervous. She delivered him to the side of the stage during the interval and then went to join his father and mother for the rest of the performance. His voice rang out clear and beautiful over St David's Hall. His performance was as professional as that of any of the distinguished soloists and when he returned to the stage to take his bow, the audience erupted in applause, and shouts of 'bravo' rang out.

Aled's reaction to all the acclaim was typically modest. 'That was the first time that I'd sung in a concert of that scale—I was pinching myself just to see whether I was in a dream or not, because I couldn't believe it. I finished singing, and because I wasn't the last thing happening in the oratorio, I had to wait there for about half an hour before we all walked on. I felt really great, and proud, but still very nervous as I wasn't sure whether they were applauding me or anyone else.'

Many newspapers gave Aled encouraging reviews on his performance:

'. . . his regrettably short account of the Angel's music could not have been more expressive.'

'. . . a brilliant treble, Aled Jones from Bangor Cathedral as the Angel.'

'. . . But the person who was to steal quite a lot of the limelight was young Aled Jones of Anglesey, who sang the part of the Angel touchingly and with great confidence for one so young at such a memorable occasion.'

John Hugh Thomas, Conductor of the BBC Welsh Chorus, gives a considered judgement on Aled's performance: 'It was clear from this, Aled's very first performance with the BBC Welsh Symphony Orchestra and Chorus, that his was a remarkable talent. Far from being overawed by having to share the platform with such

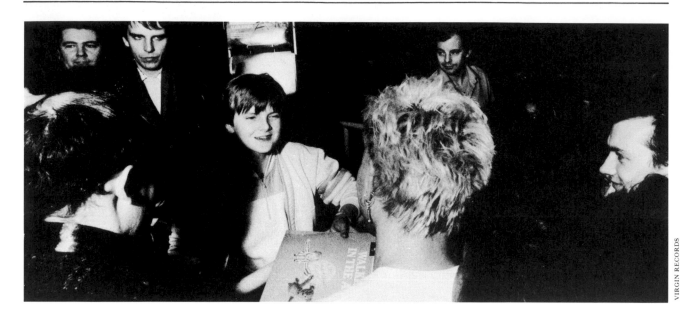

VIRGIN RECORDS

distinguished soloists as Emma Kirkby, Alfreda Hodgson, Paul Esswood, Anthony Rolf Johnson and Stephen Roberts, Aled sang his recitative and aria, "Rise Jephtha" and "Happy Iphis shalt thou live", with a poise and calm assurance that won the admiration of his fellow performers and audience alike. Though placed at some distance behind and above the large orchestra, his voice carried easily to reach every corner of St David's Hall. With this one performance, his future success was virtually certain.'

Aled's busy concert schedule would have exhausted someone with less energy and enthusiasm. After travelling down to Cardiff for *Jephtha*, Aled had to rush back home the next day to sing at a recital that evening in Bangor Cathedral, along with Robert Wyn Roberts and Julie Wynne.

About a month later, Aled worked once again with the BBC Welsh Chorus, singing, among other pieces, Mendelssohn's great motet, 'Hor Mein Bitten' (Hear my Prayer). John Hugh Thomas recalls the occasion: 'It was obvious from the moment he began to sing that he had prepared his two solos, 'Hear My Prayer' and 'O For the Wings of a Dove' with great care, and his mastery over the German text was complete. He impressed not only by the thoroughness of his preparation but by his ability to adapt his performance when required to do so. Every point made to the chorus during the final rehearsal concerning phrasing, dynamics, attack, diction, intonation and so on was meticulously noted by Aled, marked in his score, and immediately absorbed into his own performance. It was an impressive display of mature musicianship and professionalism.'

On 16 July 1984, BBC Radio 3 broadcast the recording of *Jephtha* from St David's Hall, but it was not until April 1985 that the full televised recording was shown.

CHAPTER FIVE

A visit to Israel

'One particular highlight was the two trips to Israel. There was a promotional visit for a day. I was to sing on a chat show there and to tell the people of Israel that the BBC Welsh Chorus were coming to Israel. Unfortunately, the TV crew went on strike and so I had to spend all the boring time in the Hilton jacuzzi!

   The second time was a bit more strenuous. We were there for eight days and I was singing on location for seven days. I had one day off, when we went to the Dead Sea. That was really fantastic.'

(Aled – *John Dunn Show*)

After the outstanding success of *Jephtha*, numerous recordings and visits to Cardiff followed. At one of these sessions, the BBC producer Hefin Owen told Aled of his invitation to sing with the BBC Welsh Chorus on location in the Holy Land. Aled couldn't believe his luck! The BBC would be involved in a joint production with United Studios of Israel to produce a Christmas programme featuring Aled and the Chorus singing carols at various locations in Bethlehem, to be shown on Christmas Eve on BBC2 and Christmas Day on BBC1. In the course of a week of filming, Aled and the Chorus would also record two 'network' programmes for Easter, and two public concerts were planned in Israel's largest concert venues, the National Hall in Jerusalem on 23 October, and the Mann Auditorium in Tel Aviv two days later.

   The visit to Israel turned out to be a wonderful experience for all concerned. It eventually produced three excellent TV programmes, two long-playing records and a popular video cassette, and it proved to be an important milestone in the development of Aled's career.

   To be able fully to appreciate this visit, it is essential to hear from those who took part. Rodney Greenberg was Executive Director of the whole project and his report gives a professional summary of eight very hectic days: 'I think it fair to say that really widespread recognition of Aled Jones dates from Christmas Eve 1984, when BBC2 showed *Born in Bethlehem*, a sequence of Christmas music he had recorded on location in Israel with the BBC Welsh Chorus. The programme was repeated on BBC1 the following morning and from the flood of letters sent by viewers, it was clear that, although already well known to loyal fans in Wales, Aled had suddenly broken through to a national audience that wanted to see and hear much more of him. Two further programmes in

'The little road to Bethlehem'

similar style were shown at Easter 1985, and a compilation from all three, *Voices From the Holy Land*, has since become a best-selling BBC record and video cassette.

'As the television director on those programmes, I wanted to convey the essential naturalness of Aled's musicianship. It was not going to be simple for any of us. He was to perform some world-famous religious songs, which can sound hackneyed, even in experienced hands. We were recording them in spectacular locations in Israel, to create a veritable Cook's Tour of the holiest places. Together with the Chorus, Aled would be working long hours in baking sunshine, or in some ancient church swarming with technical crew and curious bystanders. Retakes, make-up, minibus treks through the desert to the next biblical shrine—in the event, Aled thrived on the whole showbiz process and only seemed fed up when we temporarily ran out of work for him to do. So we sent him off to the Dead Sea to float in the tourist-filled brine. He returned with stories and souvenirs, eager for his next session on camera.

'People find it hard to believe me when I explain that Aled had to mime every note. Whether in a cramped grotto under the Church of the Nativity, or at seven in the morning on "the little road to Bethlehem", Aled synchronized his performance to audio tapes he had pre-recorded in Cardiff and which we replayed over loudspeakers. It was the only way we could guarantee consistent stereo quality free of extraneous noise in such diverse locations. Though he'd had no previous experience of this "playback" technique he amazed us all with the accuracy he achieved, even in close-up and with *rubato* to be negotiated. We felt that he outclassed certain much-televised superstars who may have forgotten how to take it seriously.

'Happily, his visit was not all miming. The evening of one day's shooting found him enthralling a Tel Aviv audience at the Mann Auditorium. In a nation where child prodigies sometimes seem as common as Jaffa oranges, Aled's appeal was universal—especially when, during a TV interview, he declared his favourite vocalist to be Michael Jackson.

'What I recall most vividly was the instant transition from boy to mature artist every time we went for a take. Aled would be fooling around with the clapper-board, joking with the crew. As we counted down into the music, he would moisten his lips and gaze unblinkingly into the lens. From then on, it was as though an unseen current was running between him and his audience, making this not a fraudulent bit of TV trickery but truly a performance. At the end of Schubert's 'Ave Maria' in the Church of the Nativity, tourists who had gathered behind the cameras, thinking the singing was "live", burst into spontaneous applause.

'We could have featured in those programmes the traditional "angelic choirboy" sound—pristine, cool, piercing, vulnerable and

Filming in Jerusalem. Aled's parents are in the background

Inset: the Church of All Nations, Jerusalem

somehow remote. Aled gave us something extra; a warmth and a musical intelligence that understands and expresses the meaning of the words, that knows how to phrase in long lines, and does so through a voice that is in itself extraordinarily beautiful. We must hope that those spine-chilling qualities will somehow resurface and prosper after the voice has undergone nature's change. Perhaps only once in a lifetime does a television director get the chance to preserve on tape such inexplicable, transient gifts.'

It was necessary for Aled to make two trips to Israel, the first one being the short promotional visit, followed, a week later, by the heavy recording schedule. One of Aled's singing teachers, Julie Wynne, accompanied him on both occasions and her account of their varied experiences on the second trip makes interesting reading.

'The days started very early and were for the most part rather tedious after the initial excitement of seeing a place you'd only heard about before in the Bible. Aled had to repeat scene after scene, most of them in the hot sun. We were issued with typed sheets, telling us where to be and when.

'Aled missed out on one of his free days as they arranged for him to do the chat show programme that had failed to be recorded when we came to Israel the first time. Shlommy, the nine-year-old pianist, and his father arrived at [the kibbutz] Nevé Ilan early and we were taken in a taxi to the television studios in Jerusalem.

'The first thing that struck us was the fact that the place was heavily guarded inside as well as outside. There were many young men carrying machine guns around. This was quite usual, we found out as the week went by, for wherever the cameras went [they were using Israeli equipment and crew], they were always accompanied by a group of well-armed soldiers who were quite fluent with their English until somebody asked them whether their gun was loaded or not; then they pretended not to understand the language at all.

'The television studios at Jerusalem were quite small but very impressive. The set and the piano that was available all added to the picture of a smoothly run, efficient network. Shlommy's father was over the moon about the programme and kept taking photographs whenever he could. The chat show went smoothly and Aled sang beautifully as usual. It was well received back at the hotel the next evening by the Choir and most of the hotel staff.

Left: the BBC Welsh Chorus

Aled amusing the soldiers and one of the choir at Shepherds' Fields, Bethlehem

Aled and Shlommi at the television studios

'On Aled's next free day, we had planned to do some sightseeing. Although we visited some beautiful and interesting places while Aled was being filmed on location, there was always a limit as to how far one could explore. On the Wednesday, Aled and I, together with his parents, planned a trip to the Dead Sea. We got up early that day, had breakfast, and with swimming gear all together, we waited for the bus that would take us to En Gedi, a place recommended by the hotel staff on the shores of the Dead Sea. The moment we got on, someone recognized Aled as being the guest on the chat show the previous night! He had to fight off a few ladies who were cuddling him. They also told the rest of the bus who he was, as well as informing the bus driver of the important passenger he was carrying. The scenery into the Jordan valley was breathtaking. We passed signs pointing to Jericho and Qumran, where the Dead Sea Scrolls were found. The massive red rock hills of the Judaean desert were fantastic and it seemed as though we were in the middle of the high peaks of a mountain range. When the bus passed a little monument on the road which said "Sea level", it was weird.

'It was hot! When we got off the bus, we couldn't wait to get into the sea. The beach was a shingle affair and had some showers(!) right in the middle. We got changed and went in. We didn't expect to float but

Above: time off in
Jerusalem

Inset: afloat in the Dead
Sea

we really did. It was very strange. The water was thick and greasy
about you and tasted absolutely foul but you would lie on top of the
water flat out and let the current float you away. As soon as you got
out, you had to shower the salt off or, as I found out, it dried on you like
a fine white powder.

'Again, the army made its presence known. Little patrol boats
roamed up and down. Helicopters passed overhead and we could hear
jets flying past frequently. But we really enjoyed our time at the Dead
Sea. Apart from its being a unique experience, Aled caught a very
healthy tan that day.

'The next day was spent in Bethlehem, recording. There were many
tourist shops about and Aled and I had a little time to look around. We

went into one shop because Aled wanted a Holy Land guidebook. I had impressed upon him not to pay more than the equivalent of £5 in English money. The shop was full of olivewood souvenirs, cribs, Christmas tree hangings and such. Aled saw the book he wanted and asked the price. Of course it was much too high and Aled told the man so; he then turned to me and asked why "my brother" couldn't pay. I explained what Aled was doing in Bethlehem and that he had insisted on buying a book himself about their beautiful country. After that, we couldn't get out of the shop. They were enthralled that such a young boy could sing so much by himself. When we finally left the shop, it was with various gifts such as a little card with pressed flowers from Bethlehem, bookmarks and keyrings. There was even a special blessing for "my daughter and my son" from the old man of the shop.'

CHAPTER SIX

Concerts, recordings and friends

'Waiting to go on stage is the most nerve-racking, I think. I'm remembering my words, I'm forgetting them and I'm just very nervous when the person that's introducing me goes on and on—because I know that once I'm on stage, my nerves will go. They just disappear as I walk on. I really enjoy being in front of an audience. I just come alive, really, I just love it.'

(Aled—'The Treble', *Omnibus*)

By the end of the Christmas season 1984, Aled's voice was becoming known over the whole of Great Britain, largely as a result of the BBC programme, *Born in Bethlehem*, being shown to a nationwide television audience on Christmas Eve and repeated on the morning of Christmas Day. The *Western Mail* of 24 December gave readers a taste of what was in store as far as Aled was concerned, in a report by Julie Richards:

> The voice of Anglesey choirboy Aled Jones has frequently been compared to that of an angel—gloriously pure and soaring clear as a bell! Despite his tender years, at thirteen Aled is far more than just a natural talent—a dedicated musician, he has lived for music since he was five years old and is determined to take up a musical career . . .

The year 1985 turned out to be a memorable and extremely busy one for Aled and his parents. Throughout the first few months, the *Omnibus* programme was being prepared and the Producer, Angela Pope, was present at a New Year Supper which took place in Beaumaris Church Room early in January 1985. Canon Meurig Foulkes, the Rector, explains what happened: 'I well remember a happy occasion in January 1985. It was a New Year Supper arranged in Beaumaris Church Room and, unknown to those present, I had invited Aled to sing. I can still see him coming into the room on that cold January

ST. DAVID'S HALL PRESENTS

South Wales **Echo**

POPS'85

Stuart Burrows sings

Saturday 26th January 1985

STUART BURROWS (Tenor)
with

KARITA MATTILA (Soprano)
ALED JONES (Treble)
PENDYRUS MALE CHOIR
Musical Director: GLYNNE JONES
JOHN CONSTABLE (Piano)
BBC WELSH SYMPHONY ORCHESTRA
Led by Barry Haskey
Conducted by
ROBIN STAPLETON

GERALLT LLEWELYN

Stuart Burrows

night with his cloth cap and muffler and, of course, his usual broad smile. Present on that occasion was Miss Angela Pope of the BBC in London. She had come to hear him sing and so impressed was she that I was asked to make arrangements to re-enact the occasion a few weeks later—the tables with their white cloths and floral arrangements and the same diners, pretending to enjoy the repast, but now with the addition of TV cameras. It was remarkable how everyone entered into the fun of being film extras! The result was to be seen as part of the *Omnibus* presentation "The Treble".'

On 'The Treble', Aled is shown arriving home from school one day. His mother opens the door and greets him with some marvellous news. Hefin Owen had rung from Cardiff to ask Aled to sing in St David's Hall, Cardiff as a guest on one of the 'Pops 85' series of concerts. Aled was overjoyed to learn that he was to sing with his 'hero', Stuart Burrows.

'I'd always said that I'd love to sing with Stuart Burrows, and when it happened, I just couldn't believe it—really. If my voice would have broken when I was about twelve or thirteen years old, none of this would have happened to me. I'd just be a normal, plain, ordinary boy.'

Rehearsals were filmed for *Omnibus* and Aled had the opportunity to question Stuart Burrows about his own time as a boy soprano and about how long it was possible to continue singing as a treble.

Stuart Burrows	My goodness, this brings back memories to me. I used to sing all these when I was your age as a little boy soprano.
Aled	I'd heard you had a fine boy soprano voice when you were young.
SB	Yes, you're going through the repertoire—the same repertoire that I used to do.
AJ	Well, that's what I hope to be, a tenor.
SB	How long have you been singing now?
AJ	I've been singing properly since eleven, but I've been singing since about five.
SB	You're fourteen now—how long do you think you'll go on?
AJ	I don't know.
SB	That's a difficult question really, because everybody is different. You are fortunate in a way, because you're not a very tall lad. Some boys, they grow very quickly from the age of twelve onwards—really shoot up like beanpoles, and that's what the problem is, because when you are a singer, everything grows with it—the muscles in the throat—and when they grow, the voice 'breaks', as they call it. I wouldn't contemplate singing, not for two years but four years. It depends on when the voice breaks. I know it's agony, because you want to sing, because you're musical. Mentally, you think you can do it, but your body tells you physically that you can't.
AJ	When will I know when I must stop singing?
SB	This is a very good question—it's the million-dollar question—because you find that there are times when you are singing well.
AJ	I just can't think of myself not being able to sing—having to be quiet for five years—because when I'm at home I just sing every minute of the day, something or other.

The night of the concert arrived and Aled waited nervously in the wings as Stuart Burrows gave him a heartwarming introduction. After a very warm welcome from the audience, Aled sang one of his most popular songs, Handel's 'Where E'er You Walk', and then Stuart Burrows came back onto the platform: 'We thought about something we could possibly sing as a duet together, and we decided upon César Franck's 'Panis Angelicus', which we will sing in our own native tongue, in Welsh.'

For the 'live' audience in St David's Hall that night, and the many thousands of people who watched this duet on television, it was, and still is, a very special moment. The voice of Stuart Burrows, the famous Welsh tenor, and Aled, the young boy soprano, blended in beautiful harmony, but that was not all. They created a wonderful moment of magic that will forever remain in people's memory. After Stuart and Aled had received rapturous applause, more was to follow. Stuart left the stage and Aled returned once more to introduce one of his favourite songs, 'Bridge Over Troubled Water'. Although the original version by Simon and Garfunkel has been a popular favourite for years, to hear Aled sing this lovely song, backed by a full orchestra, is an almost overwhelming experience. The song is also featured on the BBC LP, 'All Through the Night'.

On stage with Stuart Burrows

Nest, Aled's mother, described the effect the performance had on her: 'It was all fantastic–I was very emotional–more than ever, with Stuart Burrows. I don't know why, it just came over me. When he walks on stage he looks so tiny, and I say to myself, is he going to be able to do it? Will he remember his words? But he just walks on and does his stuff and that's it. The thing is, I can't believe it's Aled when he's out there. I look at him and say–It's my little boy.

'After the concert in Cardiff, coming back in the car, Aled was very quiet. Well, a word we use in Welsh is *hiraeth*–a longing for what has been. Will it ever be like this again?'

Aled sums up his own feelings: 'I count myself really lucky–I think I've had a chance to do everything that some professional soloists don't do in a lifetime. I've done it in a short space of time–a year!'

Invitations to appear in concerts, recordings and on radio and television were now flooding in. A few days after his concert with Stuart Burrows, for instance, Aled was filmed on location on the Lleyn peninsular for the HTV Wales programme *Celebration*, due for transmission later in February. And on 12 February, Aled travelled with his parents to London, to the BBC Studios at Lime Grove, to record the nursery rhyme 'Sing a Song of Sixpence' for the Agatha Christie's *Miss Marple* series on BBC1–after three hours of singing the nursery rhyme in a variety of different ways, Aled's voice was finally recorded, and played a small but significant part in one episode.

Over the Easter holiday of 1985, Aled was much in the public eye, appearing on television on a number of occasions. On Good Friday, the remaining programmes from the visit to Israel were shown. Viewers all over the country were able to see *The Road to the Cross* and viewers of BBC Wales saw *Voices From the Holy Land* as well. Easter Monday saw Aled off to London to appear on BBC's *Breakfast Time* for the first time, and the recording of Handel's *Jephtha* made in April 1984 was at last shown on television. Soon after, Aled travelled to the BBC Pebble Mill studios in Birmingham, where he appeared as a guest on *Pebble Mill At One*, singing 'Ave Maria'. Princess Anne was also on the show that day.

Soon after Easter, Aled's first video was made. On Wednesday 24 April he and his father found themselves travelling from Anglesey to Bury St Edmunds to undertake three days of recordings. Robin Scott, Director of National Video Productions, takes up the story: 'I had my first sight and, what is more important, sound of Aled Jones when he made his first broadcast for the BBC. I was then planning a programme of Christmas carols for a video recording with the Royal College of Music Chamber Choir, conducted by Sir David Willcocks, illustrated by Nativity paintings from the Metropolitan Museum of Art in New York. It was obvious to me that Aled would be the perfect soloist for this recording and I contacted him through friends in BBC Wales. Very fortunately, his free dates and our shooting dates coincided.

'It was for all of us, and I think for Aled and his father, Derek, a memorable trip to Bury St Edmunds and nothing could have been more agreeable than working with them both. Not only is Aled's voice a delight but his charming personality and modesty endeared him to everyone involved in those days of filming in Bury.

'It is sad, I think, that the range of his voice must inevitably change, but it would be wonderful to think that he might become as marvellous a tenor as he is a soprano.'

The hour-long video, entitled *Carols for Christmas*, was released in Britain and in America in time for Christmas 1985 and earned the following accolade from the *New York Times*:

Recording for video

GERALLT LLEWELYN

PICTURE MUSIC

Carols for Christmas

. . . One can enjoy this video cassette at any level – watching and listening intently, or as background music with some attractive visuals to go with it.

The art works – which include an intricately carved twelfth-century ivory cross, fourteenth-century manuscripts, paintings by Raphael, Bellini, El Greco and Manet, and illustrations by the American print-makers Currier and Ives – are catalogued in an accompanying booklet.

The chorus is, at various times, heard '*a capella*', and with organ, piano and brass quintet; the excellent soloists are Gerald Finley and the Welsh boy soprano, Aled Jones. Most of the best traditional carols, ranging from 'Hark the Herald Angels Sing' to 'Silent Night', are included; no 'Jingle Bell Rock' here! In short, this is an hour of classy, traditional holiday music and, as such, can be warmly recommended.

On 5 April the first record arising from the BBC's trip to the Holy Land the previous October was issued. The album, called 'Voices From the Holy Land', was originally pressed in an edition of a thousand copies, but it was not too long before it was selling three thousand copies a day!

On 17 June, Aled's second BBC LP, entitled 'All Through the Night', was released. Again, it was a great success; one result of the records' popularity was the BBC video cassette of the Israel trip, also entitled *Voices From The Holy Land*, which has been very popular; another was the issue of a compact disc, containing a compilation of Aled's songs from both LPs, and called 'The Best of Aled Jones'.

For the two BBC recordings, the second Sain LP and the Christmas record, Aled's accompanist has been Huw Tregelles Williams, now Head of Music for BBC Wales in Cardiff. He has written a delightful account of the various recording sessions with Aled: 'I first encountered the name Aled Jones when my colleague Hefin Owen excitedly told me of a rare "find" who would sing the Angel's aria in a performance of Handel's *Jephtha* which our Chorus and Orchestra were due to give with Neville Marriner. I remember registering the fact with relief, but then thought little of it until I attended the rehearsal at St David's Hall, Cardiff. High above the platform, next to the organ case, sat a small boy whose chief feature, at some distance, was his fair hair.

'When at last arrived the Angel's dramatic intervention in the powerful drama of the narrative, I was astounded not only by Aled's vocal prowess and technique but by his confident delivery, sure intonation and already mature musicianship. Chorus, orchestra and the other soloists immediately responded with much more than the polite applause which is customary on such occasions. To perform well at rehearsal is one thing, to do so in front of a large audience and television cameras quite another. Yet the aria was delivered at the performance itself not only with accuracy but also with much poise and style. Here indeed was a very rare talent.

'Some weeks passed before the Chorus recorded, over two days, material for three programmes to be filmed in Israel, in which Aled was soloist. My colleague Mervyn Williams had kindly invited me to play the organ at these sessions at the beautiful Victorian church of St Augustine, Penarth, which contains a very fine Hill organ dating from the end of the last century. Aled arrived and politely asked if he could try certain sections during a choral break. Although the music was straightforward, I felt an immediate pleasure at accompanying a singer with such a natural sense of phrasing and an instinctive feeling for the music's ebb and flow. When it came to the recording he was at one end of the church, I and the organ at another. I felt, however, that despite the difficulty of the distance he stuck absolutely to his approach at the rehearsal—surely a notable mark of professionalism in one so young.

'At the end he came bouncing up to the organ console, shook my hand very formally and thanked me. I retorted, very sincerely, that the pleasure had all been mine . . .

'Tea at the lovely Bulkeley Arms Hotel overlooking the Menai Straits and the wintry glories of Snowdonia. Aled seemed very relaxed as we chatted about everything but the task in hand: his favourite pop

Aled with two Gold Discs

stars, the varying fortunes of North Wales football and how he managed to do his schoolwork. His mother was there, keeping a careful though not intensive eye on how much he ate and talked, so as not to tire himself out – he really is a born extrovert.

'My favourite recollection of the day was switching off the little organ's noisy blower at last and sitting in the dark organ loft for the one unaccompanied track that remained. From the church below came the haunting strains of the old Welsh folksong 'Bugeilio'r Gwenith Gwyn' (Watching the White Wheat), beautifully sung in a performance which combined discipline with the essential freedom of folk melody. I shall never forget it.

'So to our most recent record of Christmas music. His solo tracks were recorded at a separate session at St Augustine, Penarth. Once again I felt the absolute assurance which he transmits to his accompanist and the concentration on detail which characterizes his performance. Bach's 'My Heart Ever Faithful' stands out as a particularly memorable performance. Since he had prepared his work so thoroughly, we were able to make an early finish and had an excellent Chinese meal with Aled and his parents, during which Aled displayed his curiosity on a wide number of subjects and his endless fund of jokes, much to everyone's amusement.

'As his career continues to reach dizzy heights, and the letters of admiration pour in continuously, one inevitably wonders how much longer his already long innings will last. When his voice breaks I certainly hope that he will soon be able to commence another, equally successful, career with a new voice. It would be a great loss to the world of singing to lose such a fine musician.'

Early in May, Aled was called to London for an audition with Christopher Hogwood. Aled tells the story himself: 'Decca called me to London for an audition to sing in a Handel oratorio called *Athalia*, with Dame Joan Sutherland and Christopher Hogwood, and I was really keen to get the part. It was between two boys, a boy called Nicholas Sillitoe, and myself. He'd done so many things in Covent Garden

To Aled's surprise the whole village turned out to greet him when he flew home from his Gold Disc award ceremony

opera, you know he was quite famous in London and I was coming from my territory to his territory. Really, I didn't think I had much of a chance.

'I knew Nicholas was a top opera singer. He'd had marvellous reviews in all the papers and he's got a real operatic voice. I don't think he's ever been a chorister like me. I wondered what kind of voice Decca wanted, the "chorister" voice or an "operatic" voice.

'I heard about three weeks after that I'd got the part. It was such a relief, I felt great.'

After this audition, Christopher Hogwood had felt strongly that Aled was the 'right' person for the part and liked him very much. The actual recording took place some weeks later on 29 and 30 May. Dame Joan Sutherland commented on Aled and his voice, 'Very pure, but has a great deal of character as well. He's great with the characterization of the recitatives that we've done – he's such a lovely chap – full of excitement over everything that's happened – it's wonderful to see a child who's interested in singing classical music.'

Aled was now fast becoming a celebrity, much in demand from everyone. He had to make yet another journey to London to appear on *Wogan*, and Terry recalls that occasion, when Aled sang 'Yesterday', and a later one: 'I've been lucky enough to have met Aled Jones on a couple of occasions, once when he appeared on *Wogan*, an inconsequential chat show, and once on a far more important "do", a

Royal Gala in Edinburgh. On both evenings, he entranced his audience, Royal and commoner alike, with the beauty and purity of his extraordinary voice. However, it was off-stage that he impressed me the most. I don't think I've ever met a more unassuming "star" of any age. Unaffected, self-possessed without a trace of cockiness – a young man with a great future as a singer probably – as a person, certainly.'

Four days after his appearance on *Wogan*, Aled was brought to the attention of a large viewing public again when the *Omnibus* documentary, 'The Treble', was shown on BBC1 on Friday 21 June. The *Radio Times* of that week introduced the programme:

> Aled Jones sings like an angel. His pure and plangent boy-soprano voice is an echo from the realms of glory. It has the power to move the listener deeply and directly, often to tears, as his fan mail bears touching witness. At the same time, his musical gifts excite a more judicious enthusiasm from seasoned professionals. This week's *Omnibus* film, 'The Treble', sees him through the hectic year that brought Aled from singing solos in a small Welsh cathedral choir to recording with internationally famous artists, via successful concert and television performances.

After the programme was televised, Aled and the BBC received hundreds of letters of congratulation on this fine presentation of a year in his life. He had impressed so many people by his talent and his obvious enjoyment of everything that was happening.

There was an added bonus: the *Daily Express* 'Opinion' column of 27 November 1985 was to carry the following comment:

> It is a considerable tribute to British television that our film makers have carried off four of the five top prizes in the United States Emmy Awards. These are given for non-American productions.

At the annual prize-giving ceremony in New York, the four British winners were announced, together with a special award for Sir David Attenborough. It was a marvellous surprise for the Producer of 'The Treble', Angela Pope, to hear that her portrait of Aled had won an Emmy. A press photograph shows Aled holding the coveted award for a few moments.

The first half of 1985 came to a close with the release by Sain of Aled's first 'single', a lovely ballad called 'Too Young to Know' which had been specially written for Aled by the prolific Welsh pop composer, Hefin Elis, who had produced both of Aled's Sain albums. This was backed by Paul Simon's 'Bridge Over Troubled Water', which had been a hit for the first time twelve months before Aled was born!

CHAPTER SEVEN

Requiem

'Just to think of Aled puts a smile on my face.'
(Jane Gregory, soprano)

Aled received a significant honour in being asked to sing at the Royal Charity Gala in Edinburgh in July held to raise money for the 1986 Commonwealth Games in the presence of the Queen. He was asked to sing the Andrew Lloyd Webber song, 'Memory', and he was to follow Sarah Brightman and Paul Miles-Kingston, who were to sing the hit single 'Pie Jesu' from Andrew Lloyd Webber's *Requiem*.

Aled appeared, a small figure alone on a very large stage. The orchestra began the introduction to the song and Aled started to sing. However, as the song progressed, it was evident that Aled was not his usual confident self. The next day, an unkind article in the *Daily Express* started the rumour that Aled's voice would have broken 'by the end of the week' and that he would now be able to concentrate on his football.

The real story was rather different and came out later. Robert and Julie were not involved in his preparation and rehearsals for the song 'Memory', and Aled felt very 'rushed' on the day of the concert. In the rehearsal, he had used his music copy but was told that he couldn't use it in the concert two hours later. Consequently, he was more nervous than usual before this performance: 'I had lots of nerves before this "Memory" song because I had never performed it before, but once I went on stage it was all right. Then, in the second verse, I lost the words – they just went blank, but nobody noticed. I made the whole of the second verse up and then did the third verse all right.'

In retrospect, it is not difficult to imagine how Aled must have felt, singing in front of the Queen and such a large audience and then forgetting the words. It certainly showed considerable initiative to 'make the whole of the second verse up', as he puts it!

The month of August is traditionally a holiday month, but not for Aled. On 3 August, Aled made a surprise appearance at the National Eisteddfod at Rhyl. Hefina Evans recalls it well: 'In this year's National Eisteddfod at Rhyl, the BBC always puts on a "Fanfare" Concert on the Saturday before the Eisteddfod begins. On this Saturday night, they put on a record of David Lloyd, a wonderful Welsh tenor, singing a Welsh hymn. When the second verse started, this little voice joined in and Aled walked on, singing and carrying on from David Lloyd's voice on the very same note, and went on singing the hymn. He walked on to this vast stage – everybody just went mad.

Aled in the Welsh language request programme, 'Cais am Gân'

GERALLT LLEWELYN

Left: signing autographs at the National Eisteddfod, 1985

That took some doing!

'And there was Aled – no nerves – "to the manner born", singing away. What's all this about? What's the matter with them?'

Two days later, Aled was on BBC's *Breakfast Time*, live from Rhyl, and led everyone in a verse of the old Welsh song, 'We'll Keep A Welcome in the Hillside'.

At the end of a busy week, Aled was once more off to London, to appear in a most unusual place. On arrival at the *TV AM* studios, he was taken down to the sewers to meet that fantastic superstar, the great Roland Rat! Considering that Roland had now met a proper superstar, they got on quite well, but Roland insisted on calling Aled 'Alec', which didn't please him. Still, that's what superstars have to put up with.

Aled also made an appearance on *TV AM*, and was interviewed by Mike Morris who, though normally their sports presenter, was looking after the whole programme at the weekend. 'I remember two aspects of Aled's visit quite clearly', he recalled. 'Firstly, he responded to my somewhat cheeky line of questioning with great maturity and great fluency. In no sense did he seem precocious in the manner of some of his more stage-struck peers. Secondly, I can remember the few seconds of silence when Aled had finished singing. It was not a silence born of boredom or disdain. It was a silence that nearly always follows (for a few seconds, anyway) a memorable and passionate piece of music. If it was a contest for attention, Aled won with plenty to spare.'

In September 1985, Robert and Julie taught Aled a considerable amount of new material for a Christmas record, and a Christmas television programme featuring Aled together with other soloists and readers and the Choir of Westminster Cathedral, where the recording was to take place. The finished product would be an hour-long programme of Christmas music and readings called *The Newborn King*, to be shown on BBC2 on Christmas Eve.

The recording took place over three days (25 to 27 September). To be present at a recording such as this enables one to appreciate just how much detailed planning, preparation and organization is necessary to achieve the high standard of the finished programme.

The Choir of Westminster Cathedral recorded the 'sound' of a number of carols on the evening of 25 September. The next day was a very hectic one. It began with Emlyn Williams recording four poetry readings in the Blessed Sacrament Chapel and was followed by Benjamin Luxon, Aled and the Choir recording two carols. In the afternoon, further solos were recorded by Benjamin Luxon ('I Wonder as I Wander') and Aled ('Come Unto Him'). The Choir was then filmed, processing to and from their places in the Sanctuary to a playback tape of the previous evening's recorded sound.

After a short break, Aled was filmed in the Lady Chapel singing two carols, John Ireland's 'The Holy Boy' and 'O Little Town of Bethlehem'. Now his part was over, but further items were recorded the next day by the Choir, soloists and readers. There were two songs by the mezzo-soprano, Eirian James, and four readings by His Eminence Cardinal Hume, together with a special introduction to the programme for American viewers. The programme was a great success, both in Britain and America, when it was shown at Christmas.

Benjamin Luxon, the internationally famous baritone, had looked forward to meeting Aled and working with him: 'Before I sang with Aled, my wife had gone out and bought his record, she had been so taken with his voice and singing. So when we knew that Aled and I were to work together in a Christmas programme, we both (being professional singers) were most interested to hear him in the flesh.

'I must say we were delighted to come across such a professional young man, not only with a beautiful voice, but exceptionally musical and with a wonderful feeling for words and text.'

A fortnight after the Westminster Cathedral recording session, Aled was back in London again. This time, he appeared as a guest with One Thousand Welsh Voices at the Royal Albert Hall on Saturday 12 October. Aled was given a tremendous welcome and terrific applause. After the concert had ended, a gentleman approached Aled, in tears, pressed some paper into his hand and then disappeared into the crowd. When Aled opened his hand, he was astounded to find two £50 notes there. The man had given him £100!

The first part of the week of 21 October was taken up with rehearsals for Andrew Lloyd Webber's *Requiem*, to be performed the following week. It was perhaps the most exciting challenge that Aled had ever been offered, but so much in demand was he that he had several other engagements that week. On Wednesday October 23, Aled sang before Their Royal Highnesses The Prince and Princess of Wales at Kensington Palace. And on Saturday 26 October Aled was invited to make an appearance at the London Welsh Rugby Football Club Celebration Concert. London Welsh were celebrating their centenary year and the concert was in aid of the Help the Hospices Campaign. It took place in the Royal Albert Hall and included four male voice choirs and the Philharmonia Orchestra, conducted by Owain Arwel Hughes, with Dame Gwyneth Jones and Aled as guest soloists.

The concert was a great success and the Royal Albert Hall was again filled with the sound of hundreds of Welsh voices. Aled was called back a number of times to take his bow.

Owain Arwel Hughes, the conductor, had first met Aled some years before, and had been very impressed with his voice then: 'Five years ago, my agent at the time was Arthur Owen, formerly manager of the London Office of Ricordi, the Italian publishers. He had talked a few times about his niece's son in Anglesey, that he had a beautiful boy-soprano voice as well as that something special which marked him out as a natural performer. I listened to a tape, met the boy, and agreed. Despite being a relative, Arthur's instinct and professional experience was absolutely right. The boy's name – Aled Jones.

'His subsequent rise to fame and popularity delighted both of us, and it was a day of immense pleasure for Arthur, Aled and me when I conducted Aled and the Philharmonia at the Royal Albert Hall in London. The other solo artist was Dame Gwyneth Jones.

'Much has been written and said about Aled's advanced years as a boy soprano, but this maturity of voice and personality has unquestionably helped him cope admirably with the enormous pressures placed upon him. I believe there's a career beyond that of a boy soprano, so natural is his musicianship, and I wish him well.'

Finally the time came to sing in the *Requiem* itself. The soloists Sarah Brightman and Paul Miles-Kingston, from the original performance and record, were joined by Aled, Jane Gregory, Iain Paton and Justin Lavender for the run at the Palace Theatre in Shaftesbury Avenue; there were various permutations of singers over the seven performances and Aled sang the treble part on three occasions.

Hundreds of people attended these performances, and found it a memorable experience; the *Requiem* seems to 'grow' on people after a number of hearings. Aled was quite nervous, as taking a major part in such a new and difficult work could be a daunting experience, especially when the part had already been sung quite beautifully by Paul Miles-Kingston. However, he performed with great distinction and delighted the capacity audiences.

Jane Gregory sang with Aled on two of his three performances. 'Just to think of Aled puts a smile on my face,' she said. 'These few words have not been delved for, they are the feelings and perceptions my mind has carried since meeting him during the London Palace Theatre performances of Andrew Lloyd Webber's *Requiem*.

'Word had been astir for some time of a wonderful new boy soprano. I actually beheld the "boy" before hearing the "soprano" – and loved them both. As I crept into the rehearsal I saw Aled's young figure, perched on a chair with the huge *Requiem* score on his knee. It was a lovely evening – these events can be very fraught as you can imagine, but David Caddick, the conductor, remained calm, good-spirited and in complete control throughout, which aided everybody's confidence. What struck me most was the incongruity of a young boy full of doubts and fears, who as an artist would put all these aside and perform with great maturity. I was as fascinated to watch him as to listen to him. At the end of the rehearsal, he went zestfully into the London night for an Italian meal, having just digested his Indian lunch – such are the perks of boyhood fame!

'Before the first performance, we stood together backstage, laughing about the various manifestations of stagefright! Unless you've actually been on stage and performed before the public, you can have no idea of the courage it can take. Aled found this courage, and like a real trouper he stood amidst choir, orchestra and audience and just poured out his voice with generosity, naturalness and artistry.

'We became good if transient friends that week and before we parted, he gave me his record of carols. To my own surprise, I played it over and over again, not through adulation, but through the sheer quality and beauty of the energy it created. What more can I say – the last sentence says it all.'

Apart from the performances of *Requiem*, Aled and Paul Miles-Kingston had met previously, at the Royal Gala in Edinburgh. It was interesting to receive the following comment from Martin Neary, Organist and Choirmaster at Winchester Cathedral, where Paul Miles-

STEWART FERGUSON

With Linda Evans of
Dynasty after the
Edinburgh Royal Gala

Kingston was in the Choir: 'Aled Jones has not only a remarkable voice of great beauty and strength, but also the capacity to project what he is singing. There is something infectious in his uninhibited approach, and I feel that an essential part of this charm is his Welshness, so splendidly captured in the BBC television programme about him. Aled must have been an inspiration to other trebles, and several of our own cathedral choristers chose his record as their end-of-term prize.

'It was particularly fascinating for us at Winchester to see Aled's development when we had another famous treble, Paul Miles-Kingston, singing in our Choir – the soloist in Andrew Lloyd Webber's *Requiem*. I can now reveal that I tried very hard to get the two boys together for a joint record. Although this did not come off, they met in July 1985 at the Royal Command performance in Edinburgh, and got on so well that they actually exchanged autographs!'

CHAPTER EIGHT

'Walking in the Air'

'I hate it, especially the "superstar" bit. I don't think there's anything "well done" about getting a Gold Disc. Millions of people get them, don't they?'
(Aled – *Woman's Own*, 25 August 1985)

In the early autumn of 1985, Aled was asked to record the song 'Walking in the Air' from *The Snowman*, by the composer Howard Blake. It had originally been recorded in 1982.

Aled's version was released in early October 1985, and after a fairly slow start, sales began to increase rapidly. The record was played a great deal on the radio and the prospect of a number of 'live' appearances made the record even more popular. By 10 December, the record had reached Number 37 in the charts. By 17 December it had leapt to Number 14 (the highest climber of the week) and by Christmas Eve, the record had made it to Number 5.

Howard Blake comments on its success: 'I wrote the words and music of my song 'Walking in the Air' back in 1982 for the film *The Snowman*. In this beautiful animated film, a young boy builds a snowman and the snowman comes to life. The high point is when the snowman clasps the boy by the hand and together they fly off through the night sky, and it is at this point that the boy begins the song, which accompanies their flight across river, mountains, sea and ice to the North Pole. Two concerts were arranged for the Barbican, but such was the demand for tickets that our concert promoter, Raymond Gubbay, set up a further concert at noon on the 28th December as well as one at St David's Hall, Cardiff. I conducted all these four concerts, and what a delight it was to work with Aled.

'His professionalism at rehearsal puts many adult performers to shame. He knows exactly the tempo, exactly how much rehearsal he needs. In concert, he holds the stage and charms the audience out of their seats. The notes are pure, the intonation impeccable; the rubato that of a true and very accomplished musician. He is quite simply a phenomenon.'

Although *The Snowman* was perhaps the main event of Christmas 1985 for Aled, and gave thousands of people the chance to see him 'live', millions saw or heard him on television or radio, and had the chance to listen to him on record. If, by some strange circumstance, anybody had not heard of Aled Jones before Christmas 1985, they would certainly have done so afterwards.

VIRGIN RECORDS

Aled's Christmas album had been recorded over various days in September 1985 at the Churches of St Augustine, Penarth and St German, Cardiff, as usual with the BBC Welsh Chorus and an organ accompaniment. It was Aled's first release on the '10' label (part of Virgin Records), and it attained Gold Disc status even before its official release. Within a day, the record had reached Number 50 in the charts, and in succeeding weeks it rose steadily and became a popular Christmas present for many thousands of people.

As for television and radio, Aled was hardly ever 'off the air'.

On Saturday 21 December, he featured in the BBC Wales programme, *Joy to the World*, a selection of carols and readings from many countries all over the world, and the following day BBC 1 repeated the award-winnng documentary 'The Treble' followed on Monday by a Radio 4 programme, 'Aled Jones – a musical portrait of a teenage superstar'. This was a delightful collection of songs and interviews with Aled and his parents by the popular BBC Wales presenter, Chris Stuart. Chris also showed his versatility in another direction, that of composer/songwriter, and listeners were treated to Aled singing his own song, composed by Chris, which expressed his hopes for the future.

Aled's Song.

Give me a song, the kind that young boys sing,
A song of open road and rustling spring.
Give me the time for sport and fun and joy,
For all work and no play maketh dull the boy.

These are the things I ask,
Were I to get them, happy would be my lot.
But above all there's one more plea –
Most important that, I very near forgot.
Give me the thing for which my young heart aches;
Give me a tenor voice when this one breaks.

Chris Stuart.

Christmas Eve arrived and the animated film of *The Snowman* was shown on Channel 4, though since it was made in 1982, it was not Aled singing the song 'Walking in the Air', as many TV reviewers mistakenly thought, but Peter Auty, who had originally recorded the song and was a chorister in St Paul's Cathedral Choir at the time. Later that evening on BBC2, Aled could be seen in the Christmas celebration of words and music from Westminster Cathedral, *The Newborn King*, which was also shown on American TV, and viewers then had to switch back quickly to Channel 4 to see him in the programme *Carols for Christmas*, which had been produced as a video by NVC Productions.

There were further appearances by Aled on the Welsh TV Channel S4C: on Christmas Eve, in *Carolau'r Byd* (Carols of the World), and on Christmas Day, in *Lleisiau Cymru* (Voices of Wales). Christmas was rounded off with a portrait of his life entitled *Aled Jones – Y Rhyfeddod Prin* (Aled Jones – a Rare Marvel), on 27 December.

The build-up to Christmas had been a hectic one for Aled. A few details from his diary show just what a busy schedule he had to keep. On 16 November, for example, he appeared in the morning on *Saturday*

Superstore on BBC1, and then rushed all the way back to Anglesey from London by train to appear in a concert that evening in Holyhead with the London Welsh Male Choir. He wasn't the only one to tear around the country: one of Aled's fans even travelled from Sheffield to hear him sing.

Saturday 23 November saw Aled appearing on ITV's *Wide Awake Club*, when the video of his forthcoming single with Mike Oldfield was shown; the single itself, entitled 'Pictures in the Dark', was released two days later. The following Saturday was a bonus for viewers in the south of England, when Aled appeared on the *Gloria Hunniford Show* to sing 'Walking in the Air' with a full orchestral ensemble in the studio.

On 7 December, he sang in a performance of Fauré's *Requiem* in Pwhelli. The very next morning Aled and his parents flew by plane from RAF Valley in Anglesey in order to reach London in time for the afternoon (3 p.m.) performance of *The Snowman*, which was a sell-out. Immediately after he had sung his songs, Aled and his parents were rushing to catch the train back to Wales to get home that evening.

He travelled to Dublin on Friday 13 December to appear in *The Late Late Show*, hosted by Gay Byrne. Tuesday 17 December saw his record of 'Walking in the Air' leap up the charts and Aled appeared that morning on *TV AM* with Nick Owen.

Thursday 19 December was a significant stage in his career – his first appearance on *Top of the Pops* – and the next day (Friday), Aled appeared on *Wogan*, singing a medley of Christmas carols which had been previously recorded. He then travelled to Germany the following day for an appearance on Munich television, when he sang the German original of 'Silent Night', *'Stille Nacht'*.

Aled and his family were able to celebrate Christmas at their home in Anglesey and then on 28 December it was back to London for two performances of *The Snowman*.

Sunday 29 December was Aled's fifteenth birthday. He received hundreds of cards, one of which gave him great pleasure, being signed by the whole Liverpool football team. Special birthday presents turned out to be a pair of blue patent leather shoes and a haircut by Richard Dalton and the Christmas week was rounded off with another appearance on BBC's *Breakfast Time*, this time with Mike Smith.

Quite a Christmas – quite a year! But 1986 got off to an equally busy start, with Aled receiving what was later described as 'the ultimate accolade', when he was featured on the satirical television programme, *Spitting Image*. This was recognition indeed!

Howard Blake's *The Snowman* was so popular that a special performance was arranged for Friday 17 January 1986 at St David's Hall, Cardiff, where Aled sang 'Walking in the Air', 'Where E'er you Walk' and 'The Little Road to Bethlehem', among other favourites, to an enthusiastic audience of two thousand. However, there was a treat in store. Howard Blake, who had been conducting, revealed that Aled

VIRGIN RECORDS

The Snowman   had asked him to write him a song, since 'Walking in the Air' had been such a success, and that he had actually completed it that morning on the train, coming down to Cardiff. After only half an hour's rehearsal Aled sang the song, called 'Make Believe', to round off a very successful evening.

1986 continued with a trip to Rome in early February to record the *Highway* programme with Harry Secombe in St Peter's Basilica for transmission over Easter. There are several other recordings in preparation, and countless other engagements on offer – who knows what the year may bring?

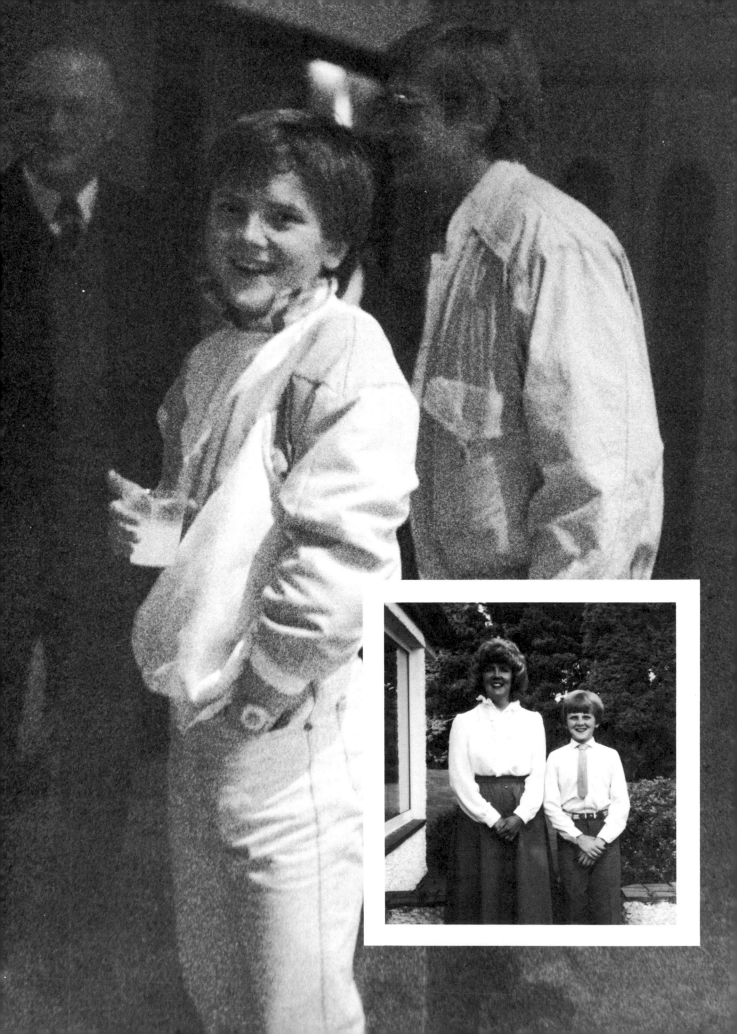

CHAPTER NINE

Aled and his parents

'I tell some of my friends that my ambition is to be a singer, but not everybody.'

(Aled – 'The Treble', *Omnibus*)

In the tremendous surge in public interest about Aled which has occurred over the past year, it is perhaps sometimes forgotten that Aled and his parents have to try and live their lives at home in Anglesey as well as coping with all the problems and pressures that fame can bring. How has this affected their lives?

Derek and Nest never thought that Aled had an exceptional voice. They knew he could sing, but never thought any more about it until people started saying things to them. They will be the first to know when his voice breaks, as it is the first thing that they hear every morning.

They had considered the possibility of sending Aled to one of the 'posh' choir schools but, Derek says, 'We dismissed it in five minutes.' Neither set of grandparents liked the idea. He is an only child and, quite naturally, Derek and Nest felt 'our lives would be empty without him'. They asked Aled if he wanted to go, he didn't, and that was that.

When his father was asked how all the fame, etc., had affected Aled socially, he replied: 'He still has quite a few friends in the Choir and the same at school, but it does make a difference to him. He's not doing the things other kids are doing – he is so committed elsewhere.' His parents have talked to him a lot and explained that it is the easiest thing in the world to become big-headed, and that's the time when people stop liking you. Aled's very good – he hasn't changed at all himself. He still enjoys all the things that other boys enjoy, although he hasn't often got the time for them.

Derek confesses all the fame has made a big change to their lives. Many weekends are spent taking Aled all over the country, and he uses up all his holidays from work – 'they're quite flexible' – whereas Nest, being a teacher, finds it difficult to get time off during term.

In the future, they hope that Aled will be happy in whatever he does, and they know that music will be in it somewhere.

At home, Aled is always singing. He'll be doing his homework and singing at the same time. If he doesn't know the words, he'll make them up, and if he doesn't sing, he whistles.

Aled with Derek, his father

Inset: Aled and Nest in their garden above the Menai Straits

He likes most sports such as tennis, snooker and swimming, and plays football when he has the time – he is a small, tough, central defender. He loves football, but at the moment singing is the most important thing in his life.

He likes listening to pop music more than classical, but sings more religious songs than pop. His favourite group is Queen and he also likes Phil Collins and Whitney Houston.

Before important concerts, he practises three or four times a week, singing scales, notes, and learning new music. He explains that Robert and Julie taught him 'the tricks of the trade' – how to pronounce words, how to 'perform' – but he is also very grateful for the training he received in the Choir at Bangor Cathedral.

On various radio and TV interviews, Aled has been at pains to point out (and complain!) that all his girlfriends are 'over sixty', but since the success of 'Walking in the Air' and his appearance on *Top of the Pops*, Aled is now in danger of being besieged by much younger girls who have fallen for his charm and good looks.

Aled loves the limelight, and still finds everything exciting. His one ambition is to be a professional singer, preferably a tenor like Stuart

With Geraint Evans at a Variety Club tribute dinner in Cardiff

Burrows. He likes performing, but if he does not achieve his ambition and become a professional singer, he may go into acting or, as he cheekily suggests, 'become a pop singer'.

At his school, Ysgol David Hughes in Menai Bridge, both staff and pupils are very aware of the success that Aled has had and they are extremely pleased that it should happen to a pupil of their school. Aled is treated no differently from the thirteen hundred other children at the school. He is accepted as a normal part of the school family. He has certainly come to terms with his fame and is seen as a normal, lively pupil, sometimes getting into trouble for running down the school corridor, sometimes pushing to the front of the dinner queue. Obviously, Aled hasn't changed, or the response of his peers would be very different. Of course, he does get his leg pulled, and nicknames such as 'Ave Maria', 'Terry Wogan', 'John Dunn', etc., sometimes fly around, together with references to his 'cassock'.

Aled himself insists on keeping his schooling and his singing separate, for obvious reasons: 'I keep my school and singing very separate because I get teased quite a lot at school. When you wear a cassock and frill and sing in a high voice, it's just something you keep from your mates. I have sung once or twice in school, but now I just feel that there's no way I'm going to stand in front of that lot and make a fool of myself.'

Aled's rise to fame has coincided with industrial action in school, and so there's been no opportunity for him to become involved in any extra-curricular activities. Otherwise, you can bet he would be involved in music and drama. In twelve months' time, Aled will be taking ten 'O' Levels, in which he hopes to do well. Many people think that he must have a great deal of time off school, but that is not the case. His parents always contact the school and discuss whether any important work is likely to be missed and they always make sure that his schoolwork does not suffer.

Aled at school is an ordinary, mischievous boy, far removed from the angelic innocence portrayed on record covers and the TV screen. At home and at school, he is able to 'switch off' completely from all the fame and frenzy of showbusiness and live an ordinary life. It is the fact that fame hasn't changed him which has made him such a popular figure among both young and old.

Epilogue
An Appreciation

'I'm not anything special . . . I've been very, very lucky and enjoyed every minute of it.'
(Aled, *Woman's Own*, 25 August 1985)

Contrary to Aled's own opinion, he *is* very special, and holds a place in the hearts of people all over the world. Aled and his parents have received hundreds of letters at their home in Anglesey. Many of these lack a proper address, and in one case it was sufficient to stick a picture of Aled on the envelope and write the word 'Anglesey'–such is Aled's fame that the letters all arrive safely. Sain Recordings and BBC Wales have received hundreds more, all expressing pleasure and delight at Aled's success. These letters show that Aled's unique, God-given talent has enriched, inspired, and (in some cases) changed people's lives. They may have listened to his voice on record, cassette or radio; seen him on television or video; or attended a 'live' performance–the result is still the same. It is interesting to find articles in Welsh language magazines which refer to Aled as *Yr'eos o Llandegfan*, the Llandegfan Nightingale.

The Reverend Ian Phelps is a Producer/Presenter for the local radio station *Leicestersound.* 'Aled Jones is a gift to a radio producer,' he comments. 'He has just so much to offer–personality, clarity, and a refreshing ease and openness. Throughout the world of radio, national and local, there are dozens of us who as producers are hoping that when the voice break comes . . . it results in the career being merely altered briefly. Aled the tenor? counter-tenor even? baritone? or bass? Whatever, it's for sure that he's made enough friends and fans to guarantee an audience.'

One person who has been able to give Aled's records a lot of 'air-time' is the Reverend Roger Royle, who, as presenter of BBC Radio 2's *Good Morning Sunday* programme, receives many requests for Aled. 'My memories of being a choirboy are none too happy. I had the unfortunate habit of singing flat and this was too much for the choirmaster, but I do appreciate the skills of those who are able to sing in tune.

'Aled Jones came to my notice when I started presenting *Good Morning Sunday*. Frequently, my producer would choose pieces he had recorded to play during the programme, and I must say I was only too pleased to do so. It soon became very obvious that it was not only me that was pleased. Hardly a week goes by without someone asking for an Aled Jones record, and, although the programme is not a request programme, it became very easy to satisfy these people's choice. The fact that most of the music he sings is religious obviously appeals to the sort of person who listens to *Good Morning Sunday*, but for me it is not just a matter of hearing a beautiful voice, it is also the joy of listening to a singer who can project the words as well.

'I thoroughly enjoy Aled's non-religious recordings, especially the current single "Walking in the Air". I just hope that when the voice breaks, it will re-settle just as beautifully in a lower key.'

At last year's Edinburgh Festival (1985), the Religious Programmes Department of Radio Forth had a daily 'spot' and Anne Pagan comments, 'One of the most moving moments on the "Pause for Prayer and Reflection" within Edinburgh Festival Radio was provided by Aled Jones, voicing the traditional prayer "O for the Wings of a Dove". Somehow, the spirit of searching and uplifting at the heart of the Festival was summed up in his clarity and sincerity.'

A similar theme comes from the Reverend Peter King of Great Western Radio: 'Aled will be familiar with the phrase from worship, *Sursum Corda*, or Lift Up Your Hearts, but for many of us who come to worship dull of mind and heavy of heart, that's too much too expect. So we depend on the voice and music of others to do this for us. Aled's is such a voice and we thank God for it.'

Perhaps one of the most beautiful tributes comes from Mrs Audrey Wilkinson on the Island of Rousay in the Orkneys: 'Here on Rousay, we have our little Roman Catholic Chapel which, I hasten to add, is open to all denominations, and as it is so small, instead of an organ we have a cassette player for hymns, etc. You can imagine how delighted we are to be able to listen to Aled singing our favourite hymns for Mass such as "Panis Angelicus", "Agnus Dei", "Ave Maria", and others too including, at Christmas, "The Little Road to Bethlehem". Recently, Aled's voice has been heard all over Orkney in a request programme on Orkney Radio, when "Bless This House" and "All Through the Night" were chosen by listeners.'

All sorts of people have been inspired by Aleds voice, musicianship and personality. Here it is only possible to include a small selection of the hundreds of stories that could be told. The well-known wrestler, Big Daddy, is one of Aled's greatest fans: 'As a wrestler, I travel thousands of miles. In doing so, I listen to the radio and cassettes. One day, while driving from Yorkshire to the Royal Albert Hall, London to wrestle in the main event against the forty-three-stone Giant Haystacks, my mind was on the problem of how to down the giant when suddenly from the radio came this beautiful boy soprano's voice, singing with a magic that

VIRGIN RECORDS

very few are ever gifted with. Magic, that's what it was. I forgot the Giant Haystacks and the big match at the Albert Hall. My brother and a friend were travelling with me. We all went quiet at the end of the recording to catch the name of the artist. The name was Aled Jones, a thirteen-year-old boy from north Wales—pure magic.'

A lady from Sheffield found Aled's voice affecting her life in a number of ways: 'I didn't know the human voice could be quite so beautiful—and I haven't heard another which retains the warmth, the full character of the voice and expression and purity in that range. It was startling to find that months have been dominated by the delight of a sound, even to the extent of hearing Aled sing 'live' rather than go away on holiday. Aled obviously really enjoys singing for people. At Holyhead on November 9, he walked in, exhausted after a long journey, seemed to relax and light up as soon as he started singing, and then sang more beautifully than ever—with his usual apparent ease, not reaching for but dropping gently onto notes.'

Mrs C. M. Burton, writing from Cornwall, says that Aled's voice reminded her of a calm, starry night on Ascension Island during the last war, where her late husband and family were stationed with Cable and Wireless Ltd. Walking home that evening, they heard the lovely voice of a young English sailor, coming across the air, singing 'The Holy City'. Aled's wonderful voice brought back this touching memory.

Mrs Hefina Evans, who first wrote to Sain about Aled's voice, visited relatives in Canada in May 1985 and took Aled's records with her. She stayed with her niece, who played the records on her excellent stereo in a large room with marvellous acoustics – the Canadians were quite overcome and couldn't believe the voice they had heard.

The 1985 Christmas edition of the *Radio Times* carried a headline, 'Aled – the voice of an angel', and David Dobson, writing from Zaragoza in Spain, echoes this theme. 'Without wanting to exaggerate, my first reaction was that this sound could hardly be coming from a mere mortal, it was more like the sound of an angel, yet at the same time intensely human. Not a disembodied, distant voice, but immediate and entreating. Apart from having outstanding natural talent, he portrayed an unusually pronounced gift for imparting the sheer joy of the music he was singing.'

Aled's voice has even reached the desert sands of Libya, where Dr Ken Hansard first heard Aled over the radio on *Outlook* from the BBC World Service. On a recent trip to England, he bought all Aled's records and tapes, but had to leave the records in England as 'the life of records in the desert is very short, even if they arrive in one piece and get through Customs safely'.

While there have already been comments from professional musicians in previous chapters, there are many opinions and comments from ordinary people on Aled's musicianship that I would like to include. Again, it is only possible to choose a few.

Valerie Austin, from Bognor Regis, feels that there must be many people like herself who have found their weary spirits refreshed by his artistry: 'Quite apart from the exceptional beauty of his voice, which is almost always perfectly placed, Aled's technique and vocal discipline is, to say the least, unusual for a boy of his age. These qualities, together with his innate musicianship, would by themselves mark him out as an artist of outstanding calibre. But there is another element, impossible to quantify or describe adequately. The Welsh lady who brought him to the notice of the recording company said that his voice "reaches to the heart" – and so it does. This ability, given to very few, makes one discard the word "talent" as doing less than justice to the truth.

'My singing teacher constantly said that the really good singer should give the same impression as a songbird which simply opens its mouth and pours out a stream of perfect sound, because it is its very nature to do so. Aled Jones comes closer to that ideal than any singer I have ever heard.'

James Dyer, a recently retired teacher from Luton, places Aled at the top of all the boy sopranos he has heard: 'I have just retired after thirty years of school teaching. During all that time, I have never met such a confident and accomplished young man, who seems to accept his great talent as though it were commonplace, not realizing that is comparable to having trained for and won an Olympic Gold Medal.

'Over the years I have heard many fine boy sopranos: Alastair Roberts (St John's, Cambridge) and Paul Dutton (Leeds Parish Church) have been memorable. I have also listened to the older recordings of Ernest Lough, with whom Aled Jones must inevitably be compared, but to my mind and ear, none have the superb quality of musicianship and calm, natural, boyish personality that pervades every recording and television performance that Aled has made. Although sadly I have never witnessed a live performance, I jealously prize the records and video tapes that I have collected, and consider myself very fortunate to have heard what I and all my colleagues consider to be the treble "Voice of the Century". Thank goodness that through the medium of recording it will be preserved for ever.'

Hywel B. Evans, an 'exiled' Welshman living in Birmingham, tells of the time, nearly two years ago, when he was spending Christmas in Cardiganshire: 'I was idly watching a TV choral programme from Beaumaris Church, feeling replete and drowsily at peace with the world, when I was suddenly galvanized into attention by the extraordinary voice of the boy soloist. It was quite unlike the conventional choirboy's voice—no breathlessness, full sustained legato singing, and an innate sense of phrasing and interpretation.

'*Diolch o galon, Aled, am y pleser 'rydych wedi ei roi i laweroedd a bendith arnoch!*' (Thank you from the heart, Aled, for the pleasure which you have given to many, and all blessings to you!)

Mike Nicholls, writing from High Wycombe, firmly believes that Aled has the finest treble voice ever recorded, and explains why he thinks this is so: 'What makes Aled's voice so good is the fact that he has tremendous confidence in his talent because it comes from an innate musical sense that is totally natural to him. He sings like you and I walk: naturally and without having to think about it. It is a well-known fact that a nervous treble is a treble in trouble. Nerves prevent accurate pitching of notes, sending a treble voice sharp. Aled always pitches his notes—even the highest ones—perfectly, and his decorative grace notes in, for instance, 'Where E'er you Walk' are always a joy to hear, both for their musical effect and for their precision.

'However, confidence and an innate musical sense are useless without a good voice, and this, for me, is where Aled scores most highly. No other performer has so readily moved me to tears with the beauty of his art. It is amazing that so young an artist can sing with such maturity and emotion with a voice that reaches straight to the heart. His joy in his unique talent springs out from the sound he makes and can catch a listener unawares: one does not grow to like his voice, he wins over the listener on the first hearing, and the universality of his appeal is evident from the popularity of his records.

'But it is only seeing Aled in a live concert that one is able fully to appreciate not only his talent but also his personality. He walks onto the stage and acknowledges the applause with a bow, accompanied by an impish smile, and he is obviously enjoying every moment. There is no sound from the audience until the song is over, and then there is thunderous applause, which he acknowledges modestly. I have so far seen him twice in concert, and each time, of all the performers on the bill, he has received the loudest and longest applause.

'The impression of his personality that one gets from the *Omnibus* programme—an (otherwise) ordinary, personable, pleasant, unselfconscious young man, blessed with a unique talent—appears to be absolutely true. He is a genuinely nice person, totally unaffected by the acclaim that his abilities have brought.'

Perhaps the most wonderful tribute comes from a gentleman from West Yorkshire who, though wishing to remain anonymous, has given permission to quote from a deeply moving and very personal letter to Aled.

Dear Aled,

I think a person needs to have heard a lot of treble voices to be able to appreciate just how wonderful yours is. I have heard hundreds of them during my life and many of them were outstanding. On many occasions during the last twenty years I have seen and heard some of the finest boys' choirs in Europe. Let me give you just once example. I have seen the Vienna Boys' Choir—the greatest boys' choir in the world—nine times in concert and I have thirty-nine of their LPs. I used to think that all the finest trebles I had ever heard were members of that choir, but all I can say now is that you stand head and shoulders above them all.

I'm sure that before long, your records will be heard and loved everywhere and then, when their day's work is over, men and women in places you and I have never heard of will sit awhile and listen to one of the loveliest voices ever heard on Earth, and they will always remember the boy from Anglesey who brought so much beauty and joy into their lives and they will think of him with great affection. And I know that while they listen, they won't mind if they can't understand Welsh.

I suppose that people will remember you mostly for your singing but I saw on your *Omnibus* programme that you have been richly blessed with intelligence, a fine personality and a rare gift for warming people's hearts. All these things have played a part in

VIRGIN RECORDS

your success and they are gifts which you will never lose no matter how old you are.

I thank you Aled for being *The Greatest Treble Ever* and I wish you all the happiness that life can bring.

After such a tribute, any others would be largely superfluous and unnecessary. It is appropriate, however, that the final words about Aled in this book should come from a Welsh Bishop, the Bishop of St Asaph:

Aled Jones, at a young age, has brought honour and joy to the Cathedral Church of Bangor, the people of Wales as well as many others throughout the British Isles and overseas. I would wish to join in the many tributes that have been expressed in recent months and to wish him every blessing in his singing career for the future.
Llongyfarchiadau a bendithion lu.

† Alwyn St Asaph.

Discography

Long-Playing Records.

1. ALED JONES – 'Diolch â Chân'
   released on both record and cassette. Sain Recordings, 1983.

2. ALED JONES – 'Ave Maria'
   released on both record and cassette. Sain Recordings, 1984.

3. 'Voices From the Holy Land' (with the BBC Welsh Chorus)
   released on both record and cassette. BBC Wales, 1985.

4. 'All Through the Night', (with the BBC Welsh Chorus)
   released on both record and cassette. BBC Wales, 1985.

   NB. Excerpts from the two BBC records have now been issued on compact disc, entitled 'The Best of Aled Jones', and on a video cassette entitled *Voices From the Holy Land.*

5. 'Carols for Christmas'
   Video cassette produced by EMI.

6. ALED JONES (with the BBC Welsh Chorus)
   released on record, cassette and compact disc. '10' Records, 1985.

7. ALED JONES – 'Where E'er you Walk'. '10' Records, 1986

   (This is a re-release of the first Sain LP, 'Diolch â Chân'.)

To be released.

1. 'Athalia' to be released by Decca later in 1986.

2. Re-issue of second Sain LP and further LPs on '10' Label.

3. Album of hymns, Telstar Records.

Single Records.

1. 'Ave Maria', BBC Records, 1985

2. 'Memory', BBC Records, 1985

3. 'Too Young to Know', Sain Recordings, 1985

4. 'Walking in the Air', EMI, 1985

5. 'Pictures in the Dark' (with Mike Oldfield), Virgin Records, 1985

Acknowledgements

Grateful thanks are due to the following people who have all helped in some way, great or small, with the preparation of this book.

Aled, Derek and Nest, for their kindness and encouragement, and Stuart Burrows, for kindly consenting to write a foreword to this book. The Controller of BBC Wales and the following members of staff: Hefin Owen, Huw Tregelles Williams, Mervyn Williams, Iwan Thomas, Chris Stuart and David Stevens; BBC, London, for permission to use programme material; Dafydd Iwan and Hefin Elis of Sain Recordings for all their help and encouragement; John Hugh Thomas, Lecturer at University College, Swansea and Conductor of the BBC Welsh Chorus; the Bishop of St Asaph; the Bishop and Dean of Bangor; Andrew Goodwin and James Griffiths of Bangor Cathedral; Canon Meurig Foulkes. Also to Annette Bryn Parri; Robert Wyn Roberts; Julie Wynne; Mrs Hefina Orwig Evans; Sir Neville Marriner; Benjamin and Sheila Luxon; David Hill; Dr George Guest; Martin Neary; Christopher Hogwood; Owain Arwel Hughes; Howard Blake and Faber Music; Jane Gregory; Richard Baker; Robin Scott; Julian Michell-Dawson; Clare Dibble; A. J. Heward Rees; Dr Gareth H. Lewis; Terry Wogan; the Reverend Roger Royle; 'Big Daddy'; Mike Morris; Edward Morris Jones; David Whittall. I am also deeply grateful for all the help I have received from BBC Radio Humberside, Radio Forth; Reverend Ian Phelps (*Leicestersound*); Great Western Radio; Aled Lewis Evans of Marcher Sound, Wrexham; the Management of St David's Hall, Cardiff; *Woman's Own*; the *North Wales Chronicle*; the *Bangor and Holyhead Mail*; the *Bangor and Anglesey Mail*; the *Western Mail*, Cardiff; HTV Wales; and S4C Wales. Last but by no means least, thanks to Valerie Austin and Romola Guiton for much help and encouragement; Llinos Davies for excellent Welsh translation; Marcus Smith and Henry Clemons for clerical assistance and Hazel Collier for technical help.

Thanks are also due to the following for providing photographic material.
Aled's parents; BBC Wales; Sain Recordings; Douglas Gowan; Gerallt Llewellyn; the Press Association; EMI Records; Decca Records; '10' Records; BBC Records; HTV Wales; S4C Wales; W. G. Rowntree; Stewart Ferguson; Gwyn Roberts.